*From the Highlands of Nkar
to the World*

From the Highlands *of* Nkar to the World

A Memoir

Martin Jumbam

SPEARS BOOKS
Denver, Colorado

SPEARS BOOKS
AN IMPRINT OF SPEARS MEDIA PRESS LLC
7830 W. Alameda Ave, Suite 103-247
Denver, CO 80226
United States of America

First Published in the United States of America in 2022 by Spears Books
www.spearsmedia.com
info@spearsmedia.com
Information on this title: www.spearsmedia.com/from-the-highlands-of-nkar-to-the-world
© 2022 Martin Jumbam
All rights reserved.
@spearsmedia

No part of this publication may be reproduced, distributed, or transmitted in any form or by any means, including photocopying, recording, or other electronic or mechanical methods, without the prior written permission of the publisher, except in the case of brief quotations embodied in critical reviews and certain other noncommercial uses permitted by copyright law. For permission requests, write to the publisher, addressed "Attention: Permissions Coordinator," at the address above.

ISBN: 9781942876991 (Paperback)
Also available in Kindle

Designed and typeset by Spears Media Press LLC
Cover photo by Cody King
Cover designed by Doh Kambem

Distributed globally by African Books Collective (ABC)
www.africanbookscollective.com

I dedicate this book to the memory of my father, Papa Mathias Jumbam, and my mother, Mama Lucela Labe. Through their ardent belief in the value of western education as taught by the Catholic Church, they ensured and insisted that we, their children, attend school, and the dividends have been bountiful.

CONTENTS

1. Nkar of My Childhood Days
1

2. Tabenken - 1963
52

3. Binju, Nkambe - 1964
59

4. Perilous Journey Down South - 1965
79

5. Buea, Historic Capital of Southern Cameroons
84

6. Man O'war Bay - 1965
89

7. Family Members
99

8. High School – 1970s
119

9. Federal University of Cameroon – 1970s
141

10. Departure For France - 1973
148

11. Back to Europe
162

12. America, Here I Come! - 1978
188

13. Canada Welcomes Me - 1980
195

14. Home, Sweet Home! - 1984
209

Acknowledgments 213

About the Author 215

CHAPTER 1

NKAR OF MY CHILDHOOD DAYS

How much of my childhood days do I remember? Not much, really. Nkar village, where I was born on the 22nd day of July in 1950, and where I spent the first thirteen years of my life, was then just a small village of a few hundred inhabitants located exactly fifty-five miles north of the German-fortified Bamenda Station on the famous but largely neglected Ring Road in northwestern Cameroon. In those days, two sometimes diametrically opposed forces rubbed shoulders with each other, at times lovingly but at other times not so lovingly. There was Nkar before any contact with the white world. Nkar of traditions, ruled over by the Fon of Nkar, the perpetrator of the centuries-old rule that streamed down from our ancestors; a rule that dictated the law, rewarded the afflicted and imposed sanctions on the guilty. Beside it, stood the recent arrival in the village, the Catholic church and its school, at the head of which sat a Dutchman, nicknamed, for one strange reason or another, "Fara Nji." He was a member of the Mill Hill Missionaries, a London-based missionary society that had taken over control of the Catholic missionary activities in the British Cameroons from the then predominantly German-dominated Pallotine Fathers.

Come to think of it, even though I am not writing about the politics that played out in the world before my birth, or shortly thereafter, it now dawns on me that Fara Nji's presence in my village carried a powerful politico-religious statement, which none of us had ever thought about. He was there because Germany had lost the First World War to Britain and France. The two victors had jubilantly shared German colonies in Africa between them. The then German "Kamerun" was one such colony which the victors sliced in two, France smilingly walking away with the bigger chunk, and Britain, taking a smaller share, which it sullenly tucked away into the underbelly of its larger neighbouring colony, Nigeria. And that is how the British (Southern) Cameroons became a forgotten speck lost in the then colonial world, which was largely dominated by the British Empire, the Empire over which, we were taught to sing in school, the sun was never supposed to set. Those were the days when Britannia ruled the waves!

One of the first decisions the British and the French took in their newly acquired colonies was to expel, not only all the German political administrators, but also the predominantly German-dominated Pallotine missionaries. That is when Rome decided to fill the vacuum left by the departing Pallotine Fathers with missionaries from a London-based missionary society, the Mill Hill Missionaries. Fara Nji was one of them and that is how he found himself the pioneer parish priest of the Saint Mary's Catholic Mission of my village, Nkar, in the late 1940s.

No one in the village seemed to know for sure who glued the nickname, Fara Nji, on the Dutchman's face but it stuck like a leech right up to the day he left the village after nearly forty years of uninterrupted stay. Wherever he happened to be – in church or out of church – Fara Nji would almost always be heard grunting and shouting: *"Cheh mabuh!"* which was always a prelude to a foot landing on some poor man's or woman's behind, or a slap slamming down on the face or head of a young child. He ruled his congregation with the rod. I always wondered if he ever knew what name the villagers called him, and why.

Floating Between Two Worlds

I knew many villagers who floated fluidly between the two worlds: worshipping in church in the morning and bowing down to the ancestral gods at night. There were exceptions, though. My father, Pa Mathias Jumbam, and my mother, Mama Lucela Labe, were among those who had their feet firmly buried in church. There was no question of any of us, their children, ever going within a hundred yards of traditional shrines, or participating, actively or passively, in any traditional practices, at the palace, where the traditional ruler, the Fon, dwelt with his family of numerous wives and children, or in other big compounds headed by powerful family heads, hierarchically ranked as *sheey, fai* or *shuufay*. That is why we grew up in our own household totally isolated from, and ignorant of, the world of traditional religious practices. When it came to church activities, however, we had to be present at evening prayers said around the hearth in my mother's house just before we went to bed. Attendance at such prayer sessions was obligatory unless one had a legitimate reason to be absent, which could only be illness or absence from the village.

Before starting primary school, children of my age first had to attend doctrine classes in preparation for the first Holy Communion. As young boys, we all knew that receiving Holy Communion was just one step closer to frequent encounters with Fara Nji as we were required to serve as altar boys. This increased our chances of being kicked in the behind, or slapped across the face, even at the height of the celebration of Holy Mass. In fact, any young boy or girl who ever came close to him stood a good chance of receiving a knock on the head with his hand, or with the big prayer book he always carried in his hand as he walked around, inside or outside the church, murmuring things from it. It was usually in the evenings that he would be seen pacing up and down the yard, his prayer book opened in his hands. We all knew better not to play anywhere near him as he would always beckon you to come nearer to be rewarded with a knock on the head. It was not rare for him to leave the altar and rush down to a pew to slap a woman who might have allowed her child to stray from her, or whose child interrupted the Mass by crying or running around loose. He even awoke one poor man during his homily with a solid slap as he was dozing off, nodding back and forth. The poor man skipped off his seat and nearly crashed into the group of women sitting ahead of him. Amid laughter from the congregation, which ceased as soon as Fara Nji turned his stern look at them, the poor man took to his heels, stormed out and was never seen in church again. The Dutchman had a good way of chasing many a potential Christian back into the waiting arms of paganism. My confrontation with him came much later, as it was bound to come.

I recall how we would walk to church in the afternoon to attend evening doctrine classes and then rush back home to draw water for the evening meal from a spring sheltered by palm bushes down the valley. We made sure we were back home before our mother and sister came back from the farm. When the day for the doctrine test came, we all lined up outside the parish priest's office and went in one at a time. It was not rare to hear Fara Nji shouting at a poor candidate for not speaking out loud enough and would often send some out of his office with a kick to their behind. If you were unfortunate to be thrown out of the parish priest's office, you would have to come back after another long year of doctrine classes. That was the only way to qualify to receive Holy Communion.

We always enjoyed loitering around the mission yard just before or after our doctrine classes taught by *Chia* Por, who was more a father to us than the tyrant the doctrine-class teachers were said to be. He was an expert in coaching and helping us to recite our lessons in our language, *Lamnso*, and it was always a delight to be in his presence. The other teachers were generally younger and less patient with us and we did our best to keep a safe distance from them. *Chia* Por was our man, our father, our coach, our consoler all wrapped into one. He knew the parents of every child in his class, and he would occasionally pay visits to our homes where he was always warmly welcomed. Before leaving, he would summon the family together for a short prayer. It was not rare to see him with a log of wood on his shoulders going to visit an old couple living alone, or a widow or widower, living all by themselves. Whenever he met a young boy or girl, who was not attending doctrine classes, he would inquire to know why; then he would ask the said child to tell his or her parents that he wanted to see the child in his doctrine classes, and many children did start doctrine classes that way.

Pa Por (Paul) Ntumpku, my catechesis teacher. Credit: Ntumpku family

I recall an incident involving a much younger catechist and my friend Dominic and me. There was a small hole behind the church, which the older altar boys said had been blessed by the parish priest and was thus so holy that no one could put a hand in it and survive. It was into that hole that the parish priest dumped the waxy remains of the candles from the altar. That was why we were warned never to put our hand into it or take anything out of it. I remember asking one of my brothers, who was already an altar boy, if that was true, and all he could tell me was that my inquisitiveness would one day land me in deep trouble. Far from quietening my curiosity, however, it fuelled it all the more, and made me more determined than ever to know what was in it.

One day, Dominic and I left our doctrine classes and began playing in the school field. We had agreed we would sneak behind the church, when no one was watching, to explore the content of the said hole. When we saw that the coast was clear and that there was no one around, we stealthily walked around the church to the hole. What we found in it were the butts of burnout candles and some pieces of paper with scribblings on them. As none of us could read, we merely tossed them back but decided to keep the broken candles. We wanted to take them home and burn them and smell the sweet fragrance of the burning wax. We were so involved in what we were doing that we did not hear the young catechist's footsteps until he pounced on us. He was screaming insults as he grabbed us each by the ear.

"What do you two think you are doing, you idiots? You dare put your filthy hands into the holy hole? Come here you two rascals; you must answer for this before the parish priest immediately!" He then firmly grabbed us each by the arm as we yelled and begged him to let us go, but he would hear nothing of it. None of us wanted to stand in Fara Nji's tribunal for we dreaded the verdict, which would inevitably be a hard knock on the head.

Fara Nji sounded audibly angry with the brutal knocks on his door, which he opened with a curse. No sooner had the door popped open than his dog jumped out from behind him and made straight for the young catechist, who was so stunned he let go of our arms and took to his heels. He was not fast enough for the dog which brought him down on the grass a few metres away. Growling and pounding down on him, it tore the poor fellow's shirt off his back and tugged on his trousers till they came loose. Fara Nji shouted to his dog to let go and the poor man skipped off the grass almost naked and disappeared into the nearby coffee farm, clutching desperately onto his torn shirt and shorts. We did not wait to see what else was coming for we took to our own heels, only stopping to take a breath when we were well beyond the parish priest's reach. We were afraid his dog would turn its attention from the poor catechist to us, but it instead went back meekly to its master, wagging its tail as it disappeared into the house. This, we observed from a safe distance near the church.

None of us said a word of what had happened to anyone and the young catechist himself deserted the parish. We later heard he had gone to his village miles away and we neither saw nor heard of him again. Days went by and we decided to put the incident of the holy hole behind us and proceed with preparations for our first Holy Communion. *Chia* Por told us that we would have to go to confession and tell the priest our sins before we would be allowed to receive the body and blood of Jesus Christ in Holy Communion.

"Look at how dirty and dusty you all are now." We all looked around guiltily at our legs and dust-covered bare feet and tried to hide them under the desks, giggling shyly. "That is how your souls are when you steal a piece of meat from your mother's pot when she is not watching, or when she steps out of the house and leaves you alone around the pot." We all giggled, guilt gnawing our entrails. He continued, "when you tell a lie, or when you hit your younger brother or sister, it is Jesus Christ you're hitting."

"But my brother is not Jesus Christ," one child put into words what we were all thinking.

"Yes, he has Jesus in him, just as you have Jesus in you." We all burst out in nervous laughter. How can Jesus be in us? The unasked question stood on every face as we looked at one another.

"Yes, Jesus loves you and he lives in everyone he loves. But you can only receive him if your soul is clean. And how do you clean your souls?" he asked, looking from one blank face to another. "You clean your souls when you tell Fada all the bad things you have done. That is when Jesus will be happy with you and you can then be ready to receive him in your souls as true sons and daughters of the church." How much of that did any of us really understand? I doubt that our good teacher ever asked himself that question.

But the mere thought of going to tell Fara Nji that you had stolen meat from your mother's pot was unthinkable! I would happily admit to Fara Nji that I hit my little brother on the head, especially as Denis was always so naughty? He would always report the least thing I did to mama, who would then give me a knock on the head or, if I succeeded to run away, she would tell me that the next time she laid her hands on me, then I would know who she truly was. We all knew such threats lasted a matter of a few minutes, and then we were all playing together in the yard.

Another worry I had about Holy Communion was the thought of eating someone's body; and how could a body hide itself inside a piece of bread?

Those were the questions without any clear answer from anyone. Maybe Fara Nji had the answers but who could ever go up to him and ask him to explain what that was all about? My immediate worry, however, was meeting him at the confessional and coming out of there alive. Even more troubling was to know what to confess as sins? It was then I remembered that each time I walked past the church, I always heard somewhere like a voice telling me "You sinned because you put your hand into the holy hole behind the church. That was a sin you must confess lest it darkens your soul so badly that Jesus will not come into it." I told the inner voice that I would. But how? I finally decided it was much safer not to bring it up, especially to the parish priest.

Then I tried to remember how many times I had stolen a piece of meat from my mother's pot. I couldn't think of any because meat was such a rare commodity that we only ate meat at Christmas. I told myself that I was still going to tell the priest that I put my hand into my mother's pot even if it wasn't meat that I stole. I had to come up with something, if not Fara Nji would send me out of there with a kick to my behind, and I would become a laughingstock of the village.

Confession day came at last. I thanked God that I was not among the first five to go into that little cubicle that was used as the confessional. We all sat outside, ears opened and directed towards the confessional hoping to pick up one or two things the others were saying. But it did not seem to be going badly after all. No grumbling or shouting from the parish priest as each boy or girl came out and walked with bowed heads directly to a seat a distance away from us. That was what *Chia* Por had instructed. Then it was my turn and, as I walked in, I inwardly prayed for the priest not to recognise me as one of the boys the young catechist brought to him and who had fled before he could hear what the complaint was. His dog was our ally and we were grateful to it. So, I went down on my knees and could see his white cassock and his sandaled feet. I could not dare look into his face even if I had not been as scared as I was for it was not polite for a child to stare an adult directly in the face. "Fara, I put my hand into the holy hole," I whispered, hoping he had not heard or understood what I said. He merely nodded his head and I wondered if he had really understood me. Then I said I had slapped my brother and made my mother angry with me. Still, he said nothing. Then I said I had stolen meat from my mother's pot. I spoke rapidly so my words would not come out clearly, especially as I spoke in *Lamnso*. When I stopped talking, he murmured something which made no sense to me except that I heard three *mshaati Maria*. So, I rushed back to the pew, buried my head in my hands and murmured three *Hail Marys*. With my sins thus forgiven, I felt sufficiently armed against any evil spirit as I boldly walked past the holy hole, making sure, however, not to look in its direction.

When Sunday came, I stuck out my tongue to receive Holy Communion from Fara Nji's hand. To my astonishment, before I could even get back to my seat, the host had already melted on my tongue, leaving a slightly sweet taste in my mouth. I wondered if I had been given the right thing at all. Why did it feel so light on my tongue and how could it melt so quickly? Later when I shared my feeling with my friends, they all said they had a similar feeling. What was even the fuss about it anyway? One boy even said he had expected a big lump, like corn fufu in his mouth. We all roared with laughter.

The post-communion celebration was rather subdued as we all went back to our respective homes where our mothers cooked whatever there was for us. My father showed rare generosity by asking my elder brother to slaughter a chicken for me. My sister, Monica, cooked rice, a rare delicacy in those days. I remember telling Denis, my small brother, that I would not let him eat my rice and chicken and he went crying to mama, telling her that I had said he would not eat my rice and chicken. For an answer, mama turned a stern look at me and I quickly got the message. Denis, understanding mama's unspoken warning, came to make fun of me, saying he was going to eat whether I liked it or not. Once the plates of rice were placed before us, we all forgot our quarrel as we dipped our spoons into our plates, laughing happily as the tasty food and chicken dropped on our tongues. What a good, sumptuous meal we all had in my honour!

* * *

Confirmation came a year later. Once again *Chia* Por prepared us for the test. This time it was much easier as we felt much more confident of what was expected of us than during the first communion period. We all succeeded in the test and were told to ensure that we took a bath, wore clean clothes and shaved our heads very low. Even if we did not have shoes, we should wash our feet and apply oil to our heads, faces and legs. The bishop was coming and let no one appear before him with dirty clothes. Did we hear that well? We all shouted our 'yes' in unison.

Before the bishop arrived a few weeks later, we made sure that the mission yard was impeccably clean. The schoolboys, many of them of a certain age already, cleared the surrounding bushes. The schoolgirls and us, candidates for Confirmation, ran back and forth to the stream to draw water that was sprinkled on the dust in front of the church and the Reverend Father's house.

On Confirmation day, the mission yard was teeming with people, Christians and non-Christians alike. Our traditional ruler himself, the Fon of Nkar, appeared to a euphoric reception from the people around. He was a tall, elegantly built, impressive, middle-aged man, fair in complexion, who moved with slow-dignified steps, nodding his head slowly as he acknowledged his people's greetings, a smile on his face. People rushed towards him from every corner of the mission yard, including children. We all forgot that *Chia* Por had warned us not to run around so as not to dirty our clothes before the bishop's arrival. The men approached the monarch, clapped both hands a number of times, letting them make a hollow sound, cupped and brought them up to their mouths, murmuring something into them. Whatever it was they were muttering into their cupped hands was not loud enough for those of us standing a short distance away to hear. Punctuating the hand clapping were voices serenading our ruler, the Fon, shouting out the names of certain ferocious animals that we had never seen but which storytellers wove into the tapestry of our folktales. I was surprised that the Fon was not angry that he was being called a "*Bvereh!*" (Lion!), "*Lum Nyam!*" (Mighty Animal!), "*Nyaar long*" (Long-horned Buffalo); "*Shuuiy Nkar*" (the Sun Shining on Nkar land), for example.

For their part, the women stooped, placing their hands on their knees, a position they maintained until the Fon went to sit at one corner of the church. That was the first time I was meeting our traditional ruler. I had only heard stories about him from some friends whose parents allowed them to visit him in his palace. Dominic, who went there often, talked of how big his palace was, how many mothers there were in the palace and the numerous children there whom no one could count. We also had with us three girls, who were the princesses from the palace. They all looked very much like their father, slender in built, fair in complexion, and just as shy around us as we were around the girls.

Our minds were still centred on the Fon and his entourage when we heard *Chia* Por's angry voice summoning us to stand in line as the bishop's car was already around the corner. We quickly formed two lines, one on each side of the road leading to the Reverend Father's house just as the bishop's car slowly came to a stop. From the back seat, alighted a tall, really massive white man in a white cassock with a big cross dangling on his chest and a small purple cap on his head.

Another white priest, who was sitting in the front seat, also came out of the car; he too was dressed in a white cassock but with no purple cap on his head or a cross on his chest. The driver, a black man, immediately packed the car at one corner, popped open the trunk and pulled out two big boxes which Father's cook helped him carry to Father's house.

On his part, Fara Nji, who was also dressed in an immaculate white cassock, approached the bishop and the other priest, beaming a broad smile. They greeted each other by shaking hands and then leaning on each other's shoulders, first to the right and then to the left and then bringing their foreheads to touch. That was new to us and I remember Christopher turning round, taking my hand and we also leaned to each other's right shoulder, then to the left shoulder and then brought our foreheads to touch, just as we had seen the clergy do. One of the church wardens leaned forward and gave our heads some smacks with his hand and we all straightened up. Then a schoolgirl, in a clean school uniform, came forward with some flowers, genuflected in front of the bishop, said something to him and then handed him the flowers. The bishop smiled at her, touched her lightly on her head, and made a sign of the cross on her forehead with his thumb. The shy girl quickly took her position in the school line, earning for herself the praises from the teachers and looks of admiration from her classmates.

As Fara Nji led the bishop and his entourage to his house, we walked in a line into the church with the school choir singing songs of praise and following us into the church. We had been told to walk in twos with both hands together as we did when praying. We took our assigned seats on the pews as parishioners rushed to occupy the other available benches. The choir, which was already well inside the church, intensified its singing which the rest of the congregation picked up and soon the whole church was singing.

It was then that we saw one altar boy walking into church, holding the crucifix, which he lifted high above his head. He was followed by the other altar boys, who walked in pairs with one of them swinging a thurible back and forth, a thin spindle of smoke oozing from some holes in its cover and spreading a rich, nose-tickling aroma which a slight breeze dispersed across the church. On reaching the foot of the altar, they stood on both sides, opening a space for the bishop and the other priests.

Behind the two priests, and to our utter surprise, came the black man, who had been driving the bishop's car, also vested in what looked like a loose-fitting white shirt over an equally white cassock. His presence sparked a short debate among us when I asked if he too was a priest. Almost immediately, my friend Dominic, exclaimed, "A priest! Are you mad? How can a Nsoman ever be a priest? Where have you ever seen that?" he asked. I thought he was right. How could I expect a Nsoman to be a priest? To us, every black man or woman had to be from Nso. I was about to add something when one of the church wardens turned a menacing look in our direction and her message came across loud and clear.

Then closing ranks behind the clergy, came His Lordship Bishop Peter Rogan himself, tall and massive to us, in full regalia, a strange cap on his head with two-spear edges pointing to the sky; in his left hand, he held an iron-like walking stick with a semi-circular head; in his right hand he waved a broom-like object in the air, occasionally dipping it into a bucket of water held by one of the altar boys. Turning to the right side of the church and then to the left side, he splashed the water on the people. As soon as the water caught anyone's face or body, the individual would bow and make the sign of the cross. That was new to us and we waited eagerly to also receive the water on our faces. Just as I was wondering what it would feel like, the water suddenly splashed on my face and caught others around me with a surprising suddenness. It felt cold on the body as we all cringed and then burst out laughing. The ever-attentive wardens turned towards us with menacing looks. One of them even touched her ear and made twisting gesture around it, indicating how our own ears would be twisted, if we did not buckle our lips.

When the bishop finally reached the altar, he gave the broom he used to asperse water on the congregation to the altar boy holding the bucket. The black man, accompanying the bishop, then took his walking stick from him and handed it to one of the altar boys, who had a white scarf hanging around his neck and reaching his knees. With the edges of that scarf, he grabbed the bishop's walking stick which he carried to his seat with much care. Then the bishop also took off his hat with its two spear-like spikes pointing to the sky, which his assistant also gave to another altar server with a similar scarf around his neck. With it, he too held the bishop's hat. Dominic, who seemed to know a thing or two more than the rest of us, then whispered loud enough for us to hear him: "You see, the bishop's hat or his walking stick should not touch a Nkar man's hand for any reason whatsoever. That is why Felix is holding the bishop's hat and Boniface the walking stick with covered hands." We all agreed that what he said sounded reasonable. None of us could imagine such holy objects as the bishop's hat and walking stick touching the hand of any of us. Those had to be holy objects that were beyond our touch. Then I remembered the 'sacrilege' Dominic and I had committed by putting our hands into the holy hole behind the church, a hole that was said to be so holy that no one could put a hand in it and remain alive. But then, we did and lived to boast about it. Were those holy objects really as lethal as people said they were? I wondered.

Before the Mass proper began, the two altar boys, the one swinging the thurible and the one with the incense boat, walked to the bishop, lifted up the cover of the thurible and the incense boat from which the bishop scooped something with a spoon-like object which he then placed on the burning coal in the thurible. A white plume of smoke oozed out of the holes on the cover of the thurible. He then blessed the thurible, which the altar boy gave to the bishop's black assistant, who in turn handed the long chains on which the thurible hung back to the bishop. That well-choreographed action amazed me. Why the backward and forward movement? I wondered. All we could see was the bishop's massive back as he incensed the altar, with thick puffs of white smoke belching from the thurible and soon a good part of the altar was enveloped in smoke. From the altar, the white smoke began to float down to the rest of us sitting on the front pews, tickling our nostrils with a rich aroma. We sniffed the air, giggling in the process as we fanned the floating smoke to our direction. It took another stern-warning look from a church warden to bring us to order.

When the Mass began, Christopher, a friend whose father was a catechist, whispered to us that the bishop we were seeing there at the altar was not just any type of bishop at all. "I am telling you the truth, I am not lying, he is the boss of all the priests in the whole world," he said, his right hand drawing a circle around us an indication that he actually meant the whole world, and not just a part of it. Christopher had to know better. He said he heard it from his father who, we all knew, was a catechist, who had travelled even to faraway Nigeria where, we were told, he had read many books to be a catechist.

***

A week prior to the bishop's arrival, *Chia* Por carefully coached us on what to do when Confirmation time came. We were to walk up, one after the other, kneel down before the bishop, who would put some oil on our foreheads with his thumb and would follow that gesture with a slap to our jaw. A slap? We all giggled at the thought of the bishop slapping us after confirming us. "Yes, the bishop is going to slap you," said *Chia* Por, "to see if you are indeed solid Christians who can now withstand torture for Christ. If the slap lands on your cheek and you start shedding tears, then you are not fit to be called a real Christian. Do you know how many slaps Christ received for your sake before being nailed to the cross? Many wicked people slapped and spat on him for no good reason! That is why you should always know that whenever you sin, or whenever you steal meat from your mother's pot, or push your small brother or sister to the ground and laugh when he or she is crying, you too are slapping or pushing Jesus. So, you must receive the bishop's slap with joy because that is how you suffer for Jesus, is that clear?" We all said yes, although I couldn't quite see the link between the bishop slapping my jaw and me slapping or pushing Jesus. By the way, how could I slap or push someone I could not even see? Those were thoughts filing through my mind and when I came back from my reverie, I heard *Chia* Por asking us to be happy and jovial. "Put on a happy face to show the bishop that you are a strong boy or girl before walking back respectfully, hands joined together to your assigned positions. Let me not see anyone changing seats after receiving Confirmation. Mark your seat well so that you go back to it with no problem. Is that clear?" We all answered, "*Ver yuni woh, baa!*" (We have heard you, papa!).

To think of a man of that size and height slapping me on the jaw was quite unsettling. That was why throughout the entire ceremony until the slap landed, I armed myself with courage and convinced myself that no matter how hard the slap landed, I would not cry. How disgraceful it would be if I were to shed a tear in front of the whole of Nkar, with the Fon himself present? My father, Papa Mathias, would add to those tears of disgrace by tanning the skin on my back with a whip. I was just reflecting on what would happen to me when *Chia* Por himself reminded us to remember that our parents would be watching us also. I looked round at my friends and knew that each one of us was nursing similar fears of punishment at home if we were to disgrace our families by crying in front of the whole village and in church, of all places.

"You all," *Chia* Por warned, "must remember to stay calm, respectful of each other and let me not hear a sound from any one's mouth! Is that clear?" He asked, slightly pulling his own ear and looking each of us in the face to show how our own ears would be pulled in case we failed to follow his instructions.

Then the moment we had all been waiting for came, and we all stood up and walked gradually and in an orderly procession to the altar, one person at a time. We went down on our knees in front of the bishop in the order we had come and he dipped his right thumb into a small saucer he held in his left hand and made a sign of the cross on each forehead, murmuring a prayer in the process, before the long-awaited slap landed on your cheek. When the first boy went down on his knees, I saw him tighten his jaws in anticipation of the slap. I thought I would hear it resound down the long church, but it did not. The bishop seemed to have just brushed past his cheek instead of actually slapping it. We all looked at each other, and I could see the same question in each candidate's eyes: 'Is that all there is to the slap?'

One girl was apparently so anxious to leave that the bishop had barely signed her forehead when she stood up and the bishop's slap missed its mark and landed on her shoulder instead. A visibly angry Fara Nji made threatening noises from behind the bishop as *Chia Por* quickly held the girl back on her knees. The bishop must have felt that she deserved a much harder correction slap for he did land a more audible smack on her jaw. All those sitting in the front pews, and who witnessed the scene, burst out laughing until a warden's stern stare restored instant order. I still felt a smile on my lips as I took the place left vacant by the visibly embarrassed girl. Then I felt the bishop's thumb scratching my forehead with some cold sticky oil, still murmuring something under his breath, and then the much-awaited slap landed on my cheek. It was only then that I relaxed the muscles around my cheeks which I had tightened in anticipation of the slap. I walked back to my seat, happy that I had not felt any pain when the bishop smacked my jaw. In fact, the idea that anyone could cry after receiving what felt like a little scratch was ridiculous. I was now a fully confirmed Catholic Christian. That feeling intensified when I later stood before the massive presence of the bishop, stuck out my tongue and felt him place the sacred host on it. I must have been in a hurry to go back to my seat for I almost knocked down the tiny saucer the mass server had held under my chin as the sacred host was being placed on my tongue. I heard the audible grunt of anger and I knew it could only be from Fara Nji. I rushed back to my seat and buried my head in my hands, more to shield my eyes from what I knew would be Fara Nji's stare of anger than for prayer. I hoped and prayed he would not come down from the altar to strike me, as he so often did whenever he was not happy with anything anyone said or did, child or adult alike.

* * *

What an afternoon of feasting we had that day! The church seemed to openly welcome some traditional dances that would otherwise have been deemed unacceptable within the sacred precincts of the church. There was the legendary *minang* dance from Rohmbii compound, which I was told was close to the palace; then the *kikum* dance from another compound, and the women's *toh* dance from the mission proper. For the first time, I could run behind some of the dancers and show my own dancing skill, which was nothing to boast of. The good thing was that I saw my parents too enjoying the show and I knew that I would not be receiving any disapproving looks once I got back home. The men's dance, the *samba-wo-mission* too moved slowly and majestically into the field, the drummers pulling the smaller drums by one hand while striking them with the other. As for the bigger drum, the *kimankar*, a young man carried it on his head while the drummer hit it with both hands as they moved into position a little distance away from the other dance groups. As soon as they took the spot assigned to them, the dancing intensified.

The whole field seemed to go into a real frenzy when the massive figure of the bishop appeared, accompanied by the two priests, Fara Nji and the other priest. The bishop's black assistant, whom we thought had to be a Nso man, was there as well. The women danced up to the clergy, bowed down graciously, wiped their feet with the horse tails they carried with them before retreating as shouts of admiration and approval rose from the crowd. The shouts rose even higher when the bishop took a few dance steps of his own towards the women before retreating. Not long thereafter, he waved to the crowd and then he and the clergy went back to the presbytery. Shortly thereafter, his car was seen driving out, with Fara Nji waving after them. He too quickly disappeared behind the blind-covered windows of his house, leaving the coast free for our people to express their joy of life through music and dance.

The dancing intensified when the Fon of Nkar, the ruler of our people himself, made his appearance. He was received by the men's group, *samba wo mission* with the drummers going into a frenzy as they frenetically pounded their fists on the drums. The dancers lifted up their spears into the skies and unsheathed their machetes from their scabbards, clashing them together in one rhythmic sound at the same time raising their voices to the heavens. Dane gunshots were let loose into the bushes, sending chickens in nearby farms and birds in the surrounding trees complaining noisily as they flew away or scampered to hide below the coffee plants.

It was then that one man, famous throughout the village for his singing, began weaving the well-known history of Nkar people in poetic renditions. He delved into a dialogue between two or more warriors, then into a monologue, followed by mimicry, before bursting out in song and dance, all in rapid succession, telling the world how Nkar had stood tall and strong against invading armies, and how our people, with bare hands, had dug trenches around their village, thus scaring the invaders away. It was then that our tall and elegant Fon, draped in a big, overflowing, neatly embroidered '*agbada*'- like gown, with big arms touching the ground, rose from his throne. As he majestically raised the arms of his *agbada* to his shoulders one arm at a time and then letting them drop right back to his sides, he took slow dignified dance steps, smiling as his people rose to serenade him. Local poets chanted the glory of his reign that was said to stream directly from our ancestors in the world beyond. With more Dane gunshots exploding in the background, the characteristic pungent smell of gunpowder enveloped the dancing ground. The women suspended their own dance and rushed forward to stand around their men, dancing and lauding the bravery of their men, who were like none other in Nsoland and beyond. Was it not their men who had always stood their ground in defence of their Fon, and the throne he symbolised, from external aggressors? Was it not their men who would take the spear in the chest as they stood like a solid rock in defence of their land and their families? Was it not their men, many now with chins as white as cotton, who would crouch like tigers on the ground, springing up at the last minute to surprise even the most ferocious beast that then served as meat for their families in times of famine! Yes, those were their men, the embodiment of courage! Men who, long after they have walked by, leave the aura of their presence clinging even onto the floors of valleys, onto the surrounding hills, onto gigantic trees, and onto the grass behind them. Yes, those were their men, united and strong like a rock, standing around their Fon, shielding him from external threats.

His Royal Majesty Fon Tume, the ruler of my people when I was growing up in the 1950s. Credit: Irinus Mbuwir (Taankar) and Fai wo Kaar

It was then that the Fon walked up to the main drum, the *kimankar*, as the drummer bowed and stepped aside, making way for his Royal Highness, the Sun that shines on the Nkar people, the Lion that roars and scares all around, the Buffalo with twisted horns on whose path nothing stands without being gored to death! The shouts that rose to the skies must have been heard dozens of miles around the mission yard. We all crowded round to see our Fon in action and he seemed to relish every minute of it, caressing the taut leather on the drum before pounding his fist on it with all his strength. In a row alongside the women, danced beautiful girls, all elegantly slim creatures whom we were told were the princesses of the palace, among whom were the girls who had been confirmed with us that morning. There is a well-known saying that if any young man is eager to see beauty in Nsoland, Nkar palace is necessarily the first port of call.

With the Fon on the main drum, poets began to weave the martial history of our people in songs that were re-echoed by the crowd to the accompaniment of heavy drumbeats, dance and song. We heard how often the *samba* war group had led raids into enemy territory, no one coming back without his machete stained with enemy blood and spears bearing the slashed heads harvested in enemy territory. Were our people not among the brave warriors of Nsoland who had faced with unbelievable courage and halted the advance of those marauding horse-back riding, bow-and-arrow armed Fulbe from the Muslim north? Those tall, lanky, long-nosed *wir mborong* (the Fulbe) came to be known in Nsoland as *bara-nyam* (horse-back riding white men). They were the battle-scarred and battle-hardened warriors, uncompromisingly loyal to that dreaded, legendary and fearless Muslim leader, Usman Dan Fodio whom, we would later learn in history, was one of Africa's most colourful, impressive and imposing religious, military and political personalities of all times. His followers had spread the word from the Koran, the holiest of all the holy books in Islam, from the north with the sword.

Legend has it that nothing ever terrified the Nso warrior as much as the sudden appearance of the horse on the battlefield. None of them had ever seen such a terrifying beast with smoke belching out of its wide-open nostrils. The Nso warriors were said to have been more terrified of the horse than of their equally ferocious and fearless riders. That was before a brave Nsoman punctured the myth surrounding the horse in an unexpected way. It happened accidentally as the said warrior was cornered by a particularly fearsome-looking beast with a sword-wielding rider descending directly on him. The terrified Nso warrior had flung his spear in despair at the approaching carrier of death and was about to flee when something unbelievable happened. That horrendous beast suddenly stopped in its tracks, tossed its rider off the saddle and came kneeling down before the astonished warrior. It was then that he realised his spear had homed in on the beast's massive chest, piercing its heart and lungs. In one swift action, he pulled his machete from its scabbard and harvested the turban-wrapped, dreadlocked head of the rider.

The mere sight of their fallen comrade, who was visibly the commander of the team, was said to have sent the others rushing back to re-group, thus giving the field advantage to their adversary, who then openly celebrated their victory because their enemy's apparent invincibility had been shattered by a brave warrior of the land. Where fact took over from fiction in such tales is open to debate; but when such elegies are being recounted in song and dance with the traditional ruler himself on the main drum (*kimankar*), no one cares about veracity or fiction.

As the dancing thickened, with the Fon expertly displaying his drumming skills, tears could be seen flowing freely from the eyes of even the bravest of men, who always prided themselves as men in whose eyes tears were never permitted to even glitter, not to mention flow, worse before their wives and children. The unthinkable was on display for all to see.

Among the men who were singing and shaking their heads as the music grabbed them, was my father, Pa Mathias Jumbam. Under normal circumstances, he would keep his distance from such traditional display of joy, equating them to pagan outbursts at odds with

Christianity. But there he was, clapping his hands and shaking his head and singing freely. Also singing and dancing among the women were my mother, my sister, my cousins and the other women from our village quarter of Mboon.

What a day it turned out to be! And to think that all that collective euphoria was in celebration of our Confirmation into the Catholic faith was truly humbling. Up until then, there had not been an instance recorded in the history of Nkar people where our Fon had left his palace just to attend a church ceremony. That he had allowed his own children to attend doctrine in the Catholic Church was an indication that he had seen the worth of the foreign religion, which he had welcomed into his land decades earlier. To him, we were all his children even if we were not all the fruits of the hard labour of his own loins. As monarch, all the children of our village were his children as well.

***

My father, Pa Mathias Jumbam, our patriarch, was decades ahead of his immediate brothers in many ways. Where his brothers, from their younger days, preferred a more sedentary life as subsistence farmers, my father, as impatient as he always was, found the lure of making money through trading irresistible. He listened to stories of those who made the long and hazardous journey to Northern Nigeria, hundreds of miles from Nsoland, with baskets full of kolanuts on their heads, or on the backs of donkeys – for those who could afford one. He yielded to the temptation of accompanying some traders on their long trek. He began by hiring his services to some of the more established traders, accompanying them with their baskets of kolanuts on his bare head for a fee. With time, however, he was able to buy his own kolanuts and became a kolanut seller in his own right. Those were journeys that sometimes took heavily-loaded traders many months on the road, covering long distances on foot through harsh territory.

It was in the course of those journeys that he became increasingly aware of the immense possibilities the world had for those who were brave enough to embrace them. He began by learning the Hausa language and mastering it well. That enabled him to better understand the Hausa people, the main consumers of the kolanuts they were selling. His fellow traders came to rely on him to serve as their interpreter.

Not only was he keen on understanding his customers, but he was also fascinated by the ease with which the Igbo from the eastern part of Nigeria dominated trade throughout the northern parts of Nigeria, and even his native Nsoland. His young mind was already interrogating the world and wondering how to also ease his way into the tremendous opportunities for growth which he saw on his journeys.

That was why when Catholic missionaries came knocking and Nsoland opened its doors wide to them. My father, unlike his immediate brothers, quickly saw behind the white man and his religion an opportunity to explore the openings to another world outside the narrow confines of his village. He, therefore, heeded their call for conversion and enrolled as a catechumen in doctrine classes. Many of them, the abled-bodied young catechumens, were often selected and sent down south, to accompany a priest who was leaving Nsoland. Their final destination was Bota in Victoria, or Bonjongo in Buea. If there was a new priest for Bamenda or Kumbo, they would also accompany him on the reverse journey. They often carried on their bare heads the heavy iron trunks those missionaries brought with them from their countries. The journey was on foot through difficult terrain, especially when they walked past Widikum and entered the thick forests of the south through Mamfe and Kumba down to the coastal regions. They were usually out on the road for weeks, if not months, depending on the weather conditions and the state of the tracks they walked on, which could hardly be described as roads.

*   *   *

Down south, he met some of his relatives, who had left their village in search of a better life at the coast. In fact, one of his half-brothers had settled in Tiko and married an Ewondo woman with whom he had two children, a boy and a girl. Some years later, when my father was no longer travelling down south, he received word that his half-brother had disappeared never to be seen again. His wife then took their children with her, probably back to her homeland, and my father never ever saw nor heard of them again. He was to die regretting that he had somewhat let down his half-brother by not bringing his family into the family fold.

News of what had transpired reached us some years later. We heard that his half-brother had reportedly joined a secret cult where human beings were exchanged in lieu of money. The story went that people given to the cult would disappear from ordinary eyes, but would actually still be alive in the underworld where they were said to work in the cult leaders' plantations. The devil was still actively alive, my father would always tell us, and asked us to steer clear of anyone we suspected could have magical powers. If we failed to keep our distance from evil individuals, he warned, we could also be kidnapped and made to disappear only to be put to work in people's private plantations in the underworld. After all, my mother would often say, when God chased Lucifer and his gang from Paradise, he did not take their power of evil from them. "So," my mother would exclaim loud and clear, "Lucifer is well and active, my dear children." That always sent a shiver through us.

Many of the people my father met down south in Tiko and Victoria worked in the large banana, palm and rubber plantations the Germans had established and which the new masters, the British, had inherited. What struck him, more than anything else, was the ease with which many of those he knew were making ready cash from plantation labour and seemingly living in great luxury. He was, therefore, determined to go back down south once he had been baptised. One of his relatives was working as a cook for missionaries in Bonjongo and he was amazed to see how well he looked and how happy he seemed with his work.

There was everything to attract him down south and he did just that upon receiving the sacraments of Baptism and Confirmation.

We always suspected that the priest, who baptised him must have given him the name Mathias, having in mind the famous passage from Sacred Scripture of how Mathias became one of Christ's apostles in replacement of Judas, the son of Simon the Iscariot, who had betrayed his master for thirty pieces of silver. The story of how Saint Peter and the other apostles had, under the impulse of the Holy Spirit, selected Mathias to replace Judas through casting lots became one of my favourite stories in the Bible.

When my father went back south, he did many odd jobs in the plantations, even serving as a house boy for a World War One veteran, who had been demobilised after seeing action in the German campaign in the defence of their Kamerun territory. When Germany lost the war to Britain and France, he and many like him, were demobilised and quickly forgotten by the new masters, who did not deem it necessary to compensate people who had taken sides with the enemy. If the British were not generous to those who had helped them defeat the Germans, some of them having fought their wars as far away as North Africa and even Indochina, why would they give a hoot about those who had been so foolish as to openly assist the enemy in his campaign against His Majesty's government?

* * *

My father finally returned from the coastal lands determined that all his children would attend school and be able to read and write so as not to face the kind of humiliation he suffered for lack of a European education. Even though the "golden fleece" was way beyond his reach, he was nonetheless determined that his children would be the ones to bring back his own share, and that could only be through the kind of education the Catholic church was giving in its schools. He became a coffee farmer and joined the local cooperative to which farmers sold their produce, the sweat of their long hours in back-breaking work in the fields, for a pittance. But that pittance did enable him to send us to the Saint Mary's Catholic primary school in our village.

For their part, my father's brothers never saw the wisdom in giving their hard-earned money to the white priest just so their children could attend school. After all, the argument went, did more useful work not reside in the farm from where food came to keep soul and body together? Why pay those lazy teachers so they could warm their butts all day long, drumming nonsensical words into children's heads, turning some of them into rebels against their own parents? My father, who could read the future with great exactitude, ensured that we all went to school and no absenteeism was ever tolerated, except for reasons of illness. School attendance became an integral part of our daily routine.

***

One thing my father seemed to have an inexhaustible store of was a package of hilarious stories about his travels down south or in Hausaland in Northern Nigeria. We would gather around him in the evenings as mama was preparing dinner to listen to him tell us about his travels. We heard the same stories over and over again and came to know them almost by heart. We would wait eagerly for him to reach funny scenes and would all burst out laughing as we mimicked the characters in the stories. We heard of how he had literally rescued some of his fellow travellers from being lynched in Hausa land because, in their ignorance of the language, they had failed to respect the boundaries of decorum required by the local traditions and customs.

It was from his stories that we heard about the way the Imams would summon devotees to prayer. He would imitate their call to prayer by raising his voice and switching the tones, lowering them or raising them high, stretching out his neck to the sky and cupping his mouth with his hands to better project his voice for all to hear. We would all scream with laughter and, in turn, imitate the different tones of his voice as well. Even though we heard the stories several times over, we all looked forward to them as they always brought so much laughter and fun in the house.

When he told stories of the long treks he and other catechumens made down south to either accompany priests going back home on leave or for good, or to accompany those priests freshly arrived in the country up to Bamenda, Njinikom or Shisong, his voice suddenly took on a more sombre and reflective tone. So many decades later, the hardships of those treks still wound their way into his voice and we came to understand how difficult it must have been for many of them to be accepted and baptised into the Catholic church. They were out on the road for days on end, only stopping to eat whatever they could find and drink water from the numerous streams they had to cross. Sometimes they were forced to wade through swift flowing rivers in the thick, impenetrable forests of the south, the water reaching up to their necks, and it was a miracle that they were not swept away by the current, especially as none of them from Nsoland could swim.

We also came to know what it was like to work in the palm, banana and rubber plantations, with mosquitoes feasting liberally on the labourers. Many of them were often victims of malaria and anyone who was absent from work for a few days, even for the legitimate reason of illness, was immediately replaced as the waiting list was long.

We also heard of what it was like to work at the Tiko wharf where they loaded steamboats bound for Calabar in neighbouring Nigeria. The waves would send the steamboats bobbing up and down, and merely going aboard with a heavy load on one's shoulders was dangerous work. He said it was not rare for workers to miss their step and find themselves in the sea, only for their corpses to be recovered days later miles away from the scene of the accident, their eyes having been gouged out by fish.

What the local labourers found difficult to stomach was the arrogance and wickedness of their supervisors, whom he disdainfully referred to as "those dirty Ibibios and Igbos" from Nigeria. He could not understand why simply because they could talk to the white man in his language, they were given the power of life and death over the local workers. It was not rare for them to cut anyone's pay at will and if you dared complain, you were sent packing immediately, some even without the remnants of their pay. The unfair treatment of the local workers hit him deeply and whenever he recounted his experiences, there was hardly any humour in his voice at all. The sombre tone of his voice would carry the repressed fury he still carried in him over several decades, and his mood would affect all of us around.

He came back home convinced that only the education taught in Catholic schools could save his children from similar humiliation in future. He would shake his head sadly and urge us to pay attention in school so that what had happened to him would not happen to his own children. "You must learn to talk and write the white man's language well so that you will hold high positions of responsibility wherever you will be working. I don't want any Ibibio or Igbo man lording it over my children as they did over me!"

***

For her part, our mother, mama Lucela Labe, had escaped early marriage by taking refuge at a local convent run by some European nuns in the village of Shisong, which became fertile ground into which Catholicism sank its deep roots in Nsoland. It was there that the white priests built a big church, a school for both boys and girls and a hospital. The nuns were always generous in receiving young girls, who were brave enough to flee early marriages that were quite prevalent in those days. My mother was just one among the numerous other girls who had also been proposed in early marriage to usually much older men, where they would join a big harem of other women. The more wives a man had, the more chances of having many children who would work his farms and bring in more harvest for the family's survival in case of famine. The man's worth was often measured by the number of wives he had and how many children he was able to sire with them.

As soon as my mother joined the nuns, she, like all the girls with her, began doctrine classes in preparation for Baptism and

Confirmation. They were also taught how to take care of the home and children in preparation for marriage. That was how my mother became a baptised and confirmed Catholic, receiving the name *Lucela* (pronounced *Luchella* in Italian). It was easy to know the origin of the nun who gave her that name.

Shortly after Baptism and Confirmation, the nuns would start the process of matchmaking between the girls and the newly baptised and confirmed men, or those about to be baptised and confirmed, many of whom were usually already of marriageable age. The matchmaking often worked and, I imagine, that was how my father and my mother met. We never discussed issues of that nature at home and I never ever asked any of them how they ever met. Such questions to one's parents in those days were unthinkable. I just assume that as soon as my father was also received in church as a baptised and confirmed Catholic with the name Mathias, they tied the knot in church. If there was one thing my parents agreed on, and remained faithful to, throughout their lives, it was the firm conviction that outside the Catholic Church there could possibly be no salvation, and that was the doctrine they hammered into our heads from the time we started walking.

To drum church teachings and beliefs into our young heads, my parents could not have had a better ally than a cousin of ours, Francis Tatah. We grew up believing that he was our elder brother. We always heard of other brothers, Kenjo, Lawrence and Michael, but we rarely saw them as they had long left the village in search of education down south. They were said to be teachers in different schools. But Francis was always there. We grew up and met him and he played the role of an elder brother very well. None of us could have imagined then that he was not our parents' son, but we only came to know much later that he was not.

He was the son of our mother's half-sister, who had been given in marriage to a head of a big family in the neighbouring village of Tavirer. It perches on one of the hills overlooking the valley that separates it from our own compound of Mboon. When the missionaries came scouting for converts, their message made a home in young Francis' heart – he was then called Tatah, becoming Francis only after baptism. He then decided to follow their teachings. His father, the patriarch of a large family, with many wives and children, declared Christianity out of bounds in his household. When young Tatah persisted, his angry father gave him a thrashing of his life, the young man only saving his life because he fought his way loose from the shackles he was tied with. His father then declared him *persona non grata* in his household, swearing that if he ever set eyes on his rebellious son again, he would kill him. The young man then remembered his aunty, our mother, and came knocking and was warmly received, given a home and treated like one of her own biological sons. In our house, he found fertile ground on which to nurture his faith. He became a catechumen and went through the necessary formation in preparation for baptism where he received the name Francis. This was before my brother, Denis, and I were born.

It was said that another missionary had come asking heads of big families to send some of their children to be trained in missionary schools. To keep the missionaries satisfied so they would leave him in peace, Francis' father surrendered his younger brother Mbinkar to them. The patriarch was apparently already sick and tired of children from a household from where a rebel had dared challenge his paternal authority. It was not uncommon for family heads to "sacrifice" their stubborn children to missionaries as a good riddance, the reasoning being that the further away such children were from home, the better paternal control could be exerted over the rest. Irony of ironies, it was usually the very sacrificial lambs who received a western-style education in missionary schools and emerged as the leaders of the new emerging country. That was the case of Mbinkar who was also received at our home. He took the name Michael at baptism. He and our brother, Kenjo, attended school and teacher training colleges together. They joined the teaching field and taught in mainly mission schools throughout British Southern Cameroons. Our brother, Kenjo Jumbam, would later find employment with the Cameroon

Development Corporation (CDC) where he worked as a teacher in its primary school in Tiko.

For his part, Francis, who never had the privilege of a western education, took to trading, buying and selling items that were in demand in households in the village – exercise books, soap, and kerosene for lamps, beans, rice and many more. He displayed them on tables outside his house and people came from every part of the village to buy what they needed for their home. With time, he also acquired a permanent spot in a weekly market in the neighbouring village of Jakiri, the biggest in Nsoland after the main market located in Kimbo, the administrative headquarters of government institutions and the seat of the paramount ruler of the Nso people. In the Jakiri market, Francis set up a big table-like structure on which he displayed his goods for sale. He would pack his wares in a big bag which he then carried on his head to the market. His economic activities began to earn dividend and he was able to buy himself a bicycle, which made the task much easier.

At home, he took his role of guardian seriously, especially when it came to matters of faith. He was always the first to arrive at the church door each Sunday morning, and would stand monitoring when we would arrive. Sunday evening, he was at the church door to make sure that we were present at benediction. If you were not seen in church, or if you came late, you were sure to stand in our parents' tribunal in the evening, and you better had a good reason for coming late to Mass, or being absent at the Sunday evening benediction service. When in church, you constantly felt Francis' eyes on your back, monitoring your prayer postures, or if you happened to say anything to a friend, you were sure to be accused of chatting in church instead of concentrating on prayers. We always felt spied on in church.

When the Mass was over, we only had one direction to take, and that was the way back home. Let it not be heard that you dared follow children, who came from the direction of the Fon's palace, the home of the "jujus" (masquerades), the pure symbols of paganism. We came to know that even if you happened to be alone in the church yard, you only had one road, the one leading home, even if friends, who lived around the palace, tried to lure you, as they often did, to follow them to their own homes.

Palace masquerades, "jujus", were not only the preserve of the Fon's palace. Individual family heads also had theirs depending on the dances associated with them. Our own family compound of Mboon, also had some but we were never allowed to go anywhere near there. Those were pagan practices only for people who had already paved their own way to eternal damnation, we were told.

***

We grew up believing that we had two sisters, Monica and Dorothy. Monica was the older one. It turned out, however, that it was only Monica who was our biological sister. Dorothy was the daughter of my father's half-sister, Kesiki, who had been given in marriage to a polygamist when she was still pretty young, as it was the practice in those days. Unfortunately, she faced mental challenges and her husband, and the rest of his household, treated her very poorly. That was when my father decided to step in. He went for her and brought her back to his own home with her two still-very-young children, Maurice and Dorothy. All this took place before Denis and I were born. We grew up seeing our father's half-sister living in a small room attached to our mother's kitchen. She was a gentle soul, spoke little and kept very much to herself and out of everyone's way. When it was time for the evening meal, mama would send one of us to bring her dish for her food. We would take the food to her with some water and she would thank us in a gentle voice.

It was only much later that we learnt that Dorothy and Maurice were her children. That Dorothy was not Monica's follower came as a shock to us. She played the role of a nanny to me and my follower, Denis, from the moment we were born until we were old enough to run around by ourselves. Even then, she was still there, playing the elder sister and making sure that nothing bad happened to us. She was the perfect elder sister and the revelation that she was not our direct sister, but a cousin, was pretty shocking. And this, we only came to know much later when we were already teenagers.

It took me several years to come to appreciate what remarkable people my parents were. They were always ready to open the door of their home to the children of their relatives and treated them just as they did us, their biological children.

Many more were to follow in later years when we were already old enough to know who was who. They too were well received and made to feel at home and we lived in peace and harmony. One example comes to mind. He was Tobias Ndze Wongbi. His mother was mama's direct follower, our aunty, who was married in Shisong, a village about ten miles away. One of her sons, Kenneth, who joined the West Cameroon police force, would later play a significant role in my life when I became a student at the Federal Bilingual Grammar School in Victoria in the nineteen sixties. Tobias was younger than me, about Denis' age. Like us, he also attended Saint Mary's Primary School in Nkar. With Denis and Tobias, I played the elder brother and we lived together with no distinction of who was who, or who came from where.

Of all my father's children, it was Monica, the only girl child, who did not have the benefit of primary education. Dorothy, our cousin, did not attend school either but it was not long after I started primary school that she found a young man, got married to him, and left for her marital home in a neighbouring village, Sop. The reason most families hardly sent their girls to school in those days was simply that the girl child was meant for marriage, and the earlier she was married off, sometimes at a very young age, the better. Several years later, my father openly admitted that he had been mistaken not to send Monica to school and apologised to her in our presence. She had graciously accepted his explanation and told him not to worry about it for the past was the past and that nothing could be done to reverse it. Even though there were girls attending primary school in the village, they were few; mainly the children of primary school teachers, who, earlier than anyone else, had seen the value of educating the girl child. I recall that some of those teachers, to their credit, did undertake a campaign to encourage parents to send their girls to school. A few parents did respond favourably to their appeal, but the majority did not. With time, however, especially from the early 1950s, more and more parents began sending their girls to the only school in the village – the Saint Mary's Primary School. By the time I started school, the presence of girls in primary school was no longer a curiosity.

Far from accepting her fate, Monica learnt to sew clothes and enrolled herself in an evening literacy education course that was taught by some teachers of Saint Mary's Primary School. Francis too, who did not have any formal primary education either, also enrolled in the same programme. They all learnt the rudiments of primary education which enabled them to function in their respective business domain – Francis as a petty trader and Monica in her sewing business. She was also very active in domestic science classes that were organised and taught by some women sent from a government unit in Bamenda. They went from village to village, training and empowering women on how to lift themselves out of poverty and engage in small-scale business ventures. They also taught the women how to keep their homes clean and what food to prepare for their children so they could remain healthy. The women were coached on basic hygiene rules, especially those of them who were pregnant or had just had babies. I remember from time to time a white woman, who was generally called "Madam", would accompany the training team from Bamenda. Monica learnt much in those training sessions and her culinary skills improved greatly. She began to cook and spice our food nicely, which we all adored.

***

Two things of significance happened in my life shortly after Confirmation. I began to attend school and, at the same time, learnt to serve Mass at the altar. Those two events became a source of great pride for me. I was, at last, gradually emerging into the world of grown-ups. Not long before then, I would leave our doctrine class in the morning and linger around the primary school to watch and admire the schoolboys and girls, some hardly older than me, marching to class in strict formations. Now, I was to be one of them and my younger brother, and others of his age, would be the ones admiring me.

Me, my sister, Monica, and Denis, my junior brother in our village of Nkar in the 1960s. Credit: Family album

Pa Anthony Tala: My Infant One teacher and later my father-in-law. Credit: Tala family

Saint Mary's Roman Catholic Primary School, Nkar. Fara Nji's legacy. Credit: Fai wo Kaar

Saint Mary's Roman Catholic Church, Nkar. Fara Nji's legacy. Credit: Fai wo Kaar

I remember vividly some of our teachers of those days who, for the most part, were already men and women of a certain age with children of their own in the same school. They turned out to be much more than just class teachers; they were also community leaders to whom many people relied for advice. Many of them had been trained in Catholic teacher training colleges either within the British Southern Cameroons territory, or in neighbouring Nigeria. What was also remarkable about them was their unflinching devotion to duty. Teaching was not a job for them, it was a vocation which they accomplished to the best of their ability. We grew up knowing that Primary Infant One was in the hands of Pa Anthony Tala, and him only. There is hardly anyone I know who attended the Catholic primary school in Nkar from the beginning who did not sit at his feet as he patiently held their trembling hand as they struggled to draw the first few letters of the alphabet on tiny slates using chalk.

I recall an incident that occurred when I was in Infant One. A friend and I had been playing in the dust in the school yard and did not realise the recess period was already over. It was the booming, threatening voice of the school headmaster, Pa Patrick Kimbo, that sent us rushing back into the classroom. Pa Anthony Tala had already assigned work to the rest of the class and stood waiting for us, a cane in hand. He asked to know where we had been and why we were coming back late. He got no answer, only frightened stares at the whip he had in hand. I doubt that he expected an answer to his question. He then held me by the wrist and gave me a whip on my buttocks. He certainly did not expect what happened next, for a thick fume of dust arose from my shorts which he received directly on his face and began to sneeze violently. He let go of my arm and the rest of the class exploded in laughter. He then asked us to go to our seats before he knocked our tiny heads against the wall, a threat we knew he had no intention of putting into action. Several decades later, I was to fall in love with and marry his daughter and add to the number of his grandchildren. Had he then known he was caning his future son-in-law, the story might be told differently.

***

As we emerged into the upper classes, Pa William Sengla (popularly known as *Chia* Wandong) was waiting for us in Standard Four. He was the school's rural science teacher, whose devotion to the school farm behind the school was legendary. He also taught us to respect and take good care of nature. Through him, we came to know not only the common names of flowers and other plants but also their scientific names that were sometimes quite a challenge to pronounce. Such names flowed fluidly from his lips and he seemed to enjoy listening to us struggle with the pronunciation.

I remember *Chia* Wandong, in particular, because, unlike most people in our village, who received the parish priest, Fara Nji's erratic and bullying ways rather meekly, including the other primary school teachers, he refused to be bullied, and Fara Nji came to know it and steered clear of him, even though it was not in his nature to openly admit defeat.

We once witnessed a confrontation between the two men that left us baffled and trembling for *Chia* Wandong. It happened that we were in the school farm with him when Fara Nji suddenly appeared on the farm. It was rather unusual for him to come around the school yard, not to mention the school farm. We were all busy planting yam tubers under the keen supervision of our teacher when the priest announced his presence with a brief cough. We all looked up in surprise. *Chia* Wandong stood up, walked up to him, rubbing his hands together to get rid of the dust. Not wanting to be caught by either man spying on them, we all lowered our heads and pretended to be very busy although we made sure we missed nothing of their conversation. It did not take long for their voices to start gaining in volume and intensity. The priest, as always, was trying to impose his views on a visibly dissatisfied *Chia* Wandong, who kept shaking his head in the negative and saying: "No! No! No! I don't agree! I don't agree with you at all!"

The priest, who probably had not expected such virulent resistance from his teacher, suddenly went silent and just stood there staring at *Chia* Wandong, who kept registering his disapproval with head shakes while staring the priest directly in the face as well. We expected the priest to send his foot into *Chia* Wandong's behind but he might have seen that his opponent would probably not have failed to retaliate and thought the better of it. Then, just as quickly as he had come, he suddenly swung round and walked away. *Chia* Wandong maintained his position, his arms at akimbo, as he watched the Dutchman's back disappear around the corner. Then he let drop his arms, murmured something to himself, but making sure it was audible enough for us not to miss a word, about not letting anyone bully him into submission. If it was appropriate, we would all have run up to *Chia* Wandong and plant kisses on his cheek. We all stood tall and proud and, before long, not only was the school buzzing with the news of the confrontation, but the entire village had heard how *Chia* Wandong had stood his ground and the parish priest had fled. Although we were sure that he enjoyed his victory over the Dutchman, *Chia* Wandong was civil enough not to openly gloat over it. Those of us hiding between the garden ridges were only too happy that Fara Nji had not recognised any of us, especially those of us who served him at the altar. As the years rolled by, echoes of that confrontation gained a foothold in the village folklore, thickening in variations as one generation after another picked up the loose ends and embellished them in their own style. One recurrent note, however, rang through the different versions of that story: the unbelievable, head-shaking fact that a Nsoman could stand his ground before a white man and win, especially when the white man in question happened to be the almighty parish priest; and not just any parish priest, the dreaded Fara Nji of all.

***

I also fondly remember the school Headmaster, "HM" as he was commonly called, Pa Patrick Kimbo. I grew up meeting him in that position. He taught the highest class in school, Standard Six, the First School Leaving Certificate examination class. That was a class of big boys and girls, some even old enough to be our parents. We all knew that it was not prudent to say anything that any of them could remotely construe as a mockery for you were sure to receive swift knocks on the head, which some of them took an obscene delight to administer to us, the school kiddies.

Pa Patrick Kimbo, the long-time Headmaster of RCM Nkar: a man of fair judgment. Credit: Kimbo family

Pa Kimbo was known to be a no-nonsense disciplinarian, who wielded the rod liberally, when necessary, but he was also known to be very fair in his assessment of situations. If you ever did anything really dumb in your class, your teacher could drag you, kicking and screaming, to the HM's office, and you were sure not to emerge from there without some strokes of the cane to your outstretched hands or your hind legs. He seemed to know the names of all his school pupils, even those who had just come in fresh into Infant One. Whenever you met him at school, or out of school, he would call you by name, affectionately touch you on your head and reward you with a smile. If you felt too shy to say anything, as it was usually the case, he would teach you what to say when an elder greeted you; and you would answer, 'Yes Sir' and either bend your head down and stare at your toes or rush away giggling.

In school, when the bell rang, either in the morning or at the end of the recess period, you would often see him standing in front of his office, observing who was hurrying to class and who was still loitering behind. You would then hear his commanding voice shouting out a pupil's name, often sending the culprit rushing back to class.

I recall two incidents involving me that made me believe Pa Kimbo' was a man of fair judgment. One occurred when I was in Standard Two and our teacher, who was still a relatively young man, seemed to have a problem with just every one of us. He therefore took pride in flogging us at a drop of a pencil. One day, he gave back some work we had done in class a few days earlier. I did fairly well in it, receiving a score of around 90 percent. In one of my idle moments, I decided to give my exercise book some colouring. I therefore used one of my colour pencils to carefully retrace his correction marks in my exercise book. Where there was a cross indicating an incorrect answer, I merely added a second layer to it; the same with the check mark indicating a correct answer. I did the same with the overall grade. As I held up my exercise book to admire my colourful artwork, he suddenly walked up to my desk and seized it from my hands. He took a quick look at my artwork and, to my amazement, began to shout at me for cheating. There he was, brandishing my exercise book in front of the whole class, calling me a cheater who had corrected his own class work. That took me totally by surprise as I had not done any such thing. Before I could even put in a word, he was out of the door soon to return with two hefty, senior pupils from one of the upper classes. They grabbed hold of me by the arms and legs and placed me tummy down on the teacher's table. He administered several strokes of the cane to my behind and hind legs. As I screamed out loud as each stroke landed, I heard my classmates laughing and drumming on their desks. I also heard the teachers in the adjacent classes asking their own pupils to either sit down and be quiet or suffer the same fate as the victim in the other room.

When the teacher seemed satisfied with his sadistic act, he literally dragged me by the ear, amidst jeers and boos from my classmates to the HM's office. Since our classroom was down a long corridor, I continued to scream in pain as he pulled on my ears. I stopped screaming when teachers from the other classes popped their heads out the door and ordered me to either shut my mouth, or they would add their own share to my agony. When he knocked on the office door, the HM asked us to come in. After listening to the teacher's explanation, he turned to me and asked if I had become a teacher to be correcting my own work.

As I was about to explain myself, my teacher brusquely interrupted me, saying that I was a liar and a bad seed in his class. Pa Kimbo asked him to let me explain myself. In-between sobs and sniffing, I managed to explain in the best way I could that I had merely added another coating to what the teacher himself had done. From the corner of my eye, I could see the teacher himself hesitating and taking a closer look at the markings. The HM himself might have noticed the teacher's own hesitation. He turned to me and said the teacher had been within his right to beat me and that what I had done was not acceptable and that if it happened again, he would himself administer the sanction. Did I hear him well? I said I did and he then asked me to go back to class. As I walked out, he said something to the teacher and they stayed back for a minute or two. When the teacher came back to class, he refrained from making any more comment, merely flinging my exercise book in my face. I sat there, with all eyes on me, some giggling, others playfully imitating my screams and whining as I had done a moment earlier. Instead of encouraging them on, as I thought he would, the teacher asked them to either shut their mouths or he would shut them himself.

What I found comforting, however, was the conviction that the HM had found my explanation credible and there was no doubt that he had, when I left them alone, made my teacher see it as well. The fact that he had asked my teacher to linger behind while I went ahead was a clear sign he did caution that monster to give me a break. From that moment until the bell announced the end of classes, he never said another word to me, nor did he encourage the others to make fun of me.

The second instance that convinced me of Pa Kimbo's fair assessment of events came when I was in Standard Four, *Chia* Wandong's class. One day during Holy Week, he summoned some of us to his office. The school senior prefect went from class to class calling out the names of those the HM wanted to see. As my name came up, I quickly made the sign of the cross, wondering what crime I might have committed. Similar questions floated in the eyes of the other pupils whose names were also called. Since it was already around breaktime, *Chia* Wandong asked us to go.

When we reached the HM's office, other youngsters were already waiting, all with silent question marks hanging from their eyes and lips. Pa Kimbo sat with his head buried in a ledger, occasionally making marks in it and behaving as if no one else was around. It was not until the senior prefect came to announce that we were all present that he looked at us, closed the ledger and stood up. Still without saying a word, he began to inspect us carefully, eyeing each one in turn from head to toe. With thick layers of dust on my shorts and shirt that had longed lost its original colour, I waited for the worse. I knew the others felt the same way because their own clothes were not in any better shape either. After he seemed satisfied with his inspection, he suddenly announced that he wanted us to form a junior choir that would sing in church during Holy Week and at Easter. We were all taken aback. We knew the senior students in Standards Five and Six were the ones who sang in church on any occasion, and some of them even taught singing throughout the school. What might have happened that made him drop them? I did not believe I could ever carry a tune, talk less of singing to a crowd, especially in church and during Holy Week of all times.

As if he were reading our minds, he suddenly said that singing in church that Holy Week would be done exceptionally by us, the younger ones. He had selected us because he had confidence in us and that he knew we would not let him down. That was some massage on our ego and we suddenly began to feel our self-confidence soar above the fear that had been gnawing us from inside as we each contemplated the enormity of the assignment he was charging us with.

It was only later that we heard what had happened; the traditional choir had been disbanded because some of its members had been surprised "doing bad things" with the girls, instead of singing. What those bad things were, none of us could say although we could only guess what they could possibly be. Some of them had even been taken to see Fara Nji who, it was rumoured, had dismissed them from school with immediate effect. The rest escaped with a lighter sentence as they were made to clear grass from the school field and around the school and the church for a whole week. As the gravity of the case was being reviewed at the level of the headmaster and the parish priest, the entire upper section of the school was plunged in silence. It was only the little ones of the infant classes who maintained their noisy nature, seemingly unaware of what was happening.

The HM's confidence turned some of us into overnight choristers, especially as he played the role of the conductor himself. We all put our hearts into the rehearsal of the songs and, barely three weeks into the exercise, we were all singing to his satisfaction. We took our song books home and practiced wherever possible. We still had to deal with the older students, who continued to taunt us whenever they could. You would have thought we were responsible for the fate that befell their colleagues. Pa Kimbo might have suspected that such threats were being made against us, or someone might have hinted him about it, for he convoked the upper section of the school, from Standard Four to Standard Six, and warned that threats against us, open or veiled, would not be tolerated. That was how we were given the peace we needed to practice singing for the Holy Week celebration. It would seem our performance did not go unnoticed, even the parish priest himself, not known for ever expressing any feeling, except anger, rewarded us with a rare smile. The HM felt pleased that we had not let him down, especially as the parish priest himself had openly appreciated our performance.

***

Shortly after receiving Holy Communion and Confirmation, some of us, the boys, were called up for training as Mass servers. What a pride it would be to kneel beside the priest at the altar and recite the prayers we so often heard the older boys recite, and in Latin to boot. I always admired the choreography at Mass, the altar boys walking up to the altar from the sacristy in twos ahead of the priest. When they reached the foot of the altar, one of them would go to the right side of the altar while the other one would step aside to let the priest pass; then they would genuflect with the right knee touching the ground, as the priest either genuflected too or merely bowed before going up to the altar. The altar boy to the priest's left had an important role to play. It was he who either placed a cushion for the priest to kneel on, or move it out of the way each time the priest stood up to go up to the altar.

The prayer at Mass was all in Latin and how beautiful those prayers sounded to our ears! No one knew what was being said but you felt them penetrating your inner being, if you did not let distraction take hold of you, which often happened to us, the young ones. I loved to see the altar boys, bowing their heads and then swaying from side to side, striking their chest and exclaiming: '*mea culpa, mea culpa, mea maxima* culpa' (through my fault, through my fault, through my most grievous fault).

I knew many of those prayers by heart even before receiving Holy Communion. My elder brothers, Boniface and Joseph, were already altar boys and I enjoyed reciting those prayers with them at home. The formal training was therefore just a mere formality for me and before long I was even assisting our formators and forming some of my classmates, who had difficulty with the Mass prayers.

When the day came for us to be tested to see if we were apt to serve at Mass, we met a different white priest, who was said to be from Shisong parish. He was much younger than Fara Nji and the two men seemed to speak the same language, which was not English. Unlike Fara Nji, who was always bubbling over with impatience, his confrere was much gentler in his ways and seemed to have a ready smile for everyone, which made him much more approachable. He was around the parish for over a month and we were told that he was there to replace Fara Nji, who had suddenly disappeared from sight. We hoped and prayed never to see his face again so the younger priest could replace him.

Luck did not smile on us, however, for Fara Nji was soon back, looking much slimmer and well groomed. He even sounded much more jovial than before and we all wondered if that was a sign of better days ahead. But, since old habits are not easy to get rid of, he was soon back to his old ways, screaming at nothing and at everything in sight, distributing kicks to people's behinds with the same generosity, worse of all to the elderly men and women before whose grey hair we were all expected to stand and bow.

One of those elderly women proved a hard nut for even a disciplinarian of Fara Nji's stature to crack. She spent just about all her day in church, never on one of the pews, where she could be easily seen, but on her knees hidden beside a pew, like a Muslim at worship. Being a woman of diminutive stature, she was hard to spot among the pews, especially towards evening when the church was dim.

One day, Fara Nji came to lock the church doors in the evening as he always did after checking to make sure that no one was left behind. No sooner had he taken a few steps towards his house than he heard frantic knocks on the main door followed by screams for help from inside the church. God alone knew what thoughts must have been racing through the Dutchman's head as he hurried back to open the door. For a second, he could not clearly see the diminutive form of the woman as she glided past him as he held the door open. He was so stunned that he did not know what to do to her, his right foot, which he raised so readily to distribute kicks to people's behind, seemingly too astonished to act. He then decided to just warn her not to stay that late in church anymore.

From then on, he decided to check well before locking the doors but somehow when he thought the search had been thorough, the same thing would happen with frantic banging on the door with the same woman gliding stealthily out the church door and making herself smaller than her already tiny form. The enraged parish priest would again scream his head off as the poor widow wiped the dust from his foot to her behind as she disappeared into the night.

This went on for days until the baffled parish priest finally decided that he needed help. He assigned one young catechist to the task with firm instructions to thoroughly search every corner of the church before locking the doors for the evening. The young man went to work and succeeded to throw the persistent widow out a few times before locking the doors. Then one evening, after what he deemed a thorough search, he bolted the church doors and went home. Fara Nji was standing outside his house when he again heard frantic banging and screaming from inside the church. Swearing and vowing to discipline his catechist, he rushed to open the church door and, lo and behold, the poor dwarfish woman glided out, her back scraping the church walls as she waited for the Dutchman to reward her behind with another kick.

It was the next day that the foot landed, not on the poor woman's behind, but on the frightened catechist's backside, who was given a sack on the spot for gross dereliction of duty. It was said the parish priest only succeeded to get rid of the woman by locking the church doors much earlier than usual. To this day, the story is still being told of how an obstinate parish priest had failed to dislodge an old widow from church, a clear indication, if any were needed, that our Blessed Virgin Mary, the Mother of our Lord, had snubbed the arrogance and self-righteousness of a priest and thrown her lot behind a poor widow, whose only fault seemed to have been her desperate search for Our Lady's divine face in the dark interior of our parish church. And was it not inconceivable, her supporters loudly asserted, that a priest could dare to toss her out of church. Did Christ, who was conceived by the will of the Holy Spirit, and born of Our Lady, not always reward the orphan and the widow and punish the arrogance of the Scribes and the Pharisees of this world, Fara Nji being a typical example? Woe betides those who, like the parish priest, deprived a poor widow of a chance to commune with Our Lady and her Beloved Son, Jesus Christ. There were, of course, those who sided with the parish priest, praising him for doing what was right and wondering why a stubborn woman had decided to make the church her home. When she stayed so long in church, they wondered, when did she have the time to take care of her own children?

***

I also had my own share of worries with our parish priest. One Sunday evening at benediction, I was one of the altar boys assisting him. It was my role to pick up the doughy cushion on which he knelt when he stood to go up to the altar to bless the people with the monstrance containing the sacred host, representing Christ. I must have been a little inattentive because I did not realise it was already time for him to go up to the altar. The other altar boy to his right realised my inattention and bent down to pick up the cushion himself. That was just the moment I too bent down to pick it up. As we tugged on the doughy cushion, Fara Nji stubbed his foot on it and nearly landed nose first on the altar. An audible expression of shock could be heard running through the entire church. As he swung round abruptly to face me, my jaws stiffened in anticipation of the fist blow or the kick I knew was surely coming. Beads of sweat formed instantly on my forehead and I could feel some of it coursing down my face and my neck. Then, just as abruptly as he had turned towards me, he turned back and went up to the altar.

Since we were all backing the congregation, as was the practice in those days, I could only hear the muffled noises that came from behind and I could tell, without seeing them, that the congregation had also expected to see me receive an exemplary correction. I was still expecting to be beaten in the sacristy after the benediction service but, to everyone's surprise, Fara Nji, very much unlike himself, royally ignored me, even walking past by as if I did not exist. One of the altar boys walked up to give me hi-five, which I reluctantly accepted, shocked as I still was from that near miss. "You have scored a victory against Fara Nji," he said as we walked out of the sacristy, disbelief still fondling my jaw where the slap could have landed.

Before long the whole village was buzzing with the news of my encounter with the parish priest. As days went by, another version even claimed that they had seen me deliberately kick the priest on the foot which was what nearly sent him crashing onto the ground. To some villagers, I had committed an unpardonable sacrilege by sending my foot out to trip God's messenger, nearly sending him crashing to the ground. Someone even gave credit to the catechist who reportedly was present at the altar – no one would say what he was doing there – and who had agilely rescued the parish priest from breaking his nose on the floor. There were, however, those who congratulated me and expressed regret that I had not succeeded to floor the Dutchman. A few of the pranksters even opted to coach me in case I needed a better tactic in future not to miss him.

The version that I deliberately tripped the parish priest was the one that reached my father's ears. Before I arrived back home, he was waiting, a cane in hand. How could his son bring such shame to his family? It took my mother's timely intervention to save me from a thrashing. She insisted, "why don't you first find out from the boy what really happened before you blame him." A good thing too that my cousin, Felix, who was serving at benediction with me, and who had attempted to pick up the cushion at the same time as I was reaching for it, explained in detail what actually happened before I was spared a strong paternal correction.

From that day, Mass serving became a scary venture for me and, up until I left the village, I only served under Fara Nji when I had no choice. I refrained from volunteering to serve at Mass for others, as it was common practice when a programmed mass server was not present for any reason whatsoever.

CHAPTER 2

TABENKEN - 1963

I left Saint Mary's after Standard Four when one of my elder brothers, Lawrence, a teacher himself, who had just graduated from the Regina Pacis Teacher Training College in Mutengene, way down south, was sent to the Catholic primary school in Tabenken in Nkambe, north of Nsoland. Instead of heading south, as many people did when they left our village, I instead headed north into Wimbum land. I expected to encounter communication difficulties, especially as I spoke neither Pidgin English nor Limbum, the local language which, I was told, was totally different from the Lamnso I had spoken all my life.

But no sooner had we arrived in Tabenken than I began to feel at home. Many of my classmates spoke relatively good English – or what we then considered standard English – and a good number of people in town spoke Lamnso perfectly well. In fact, before long everyone seemed to know me in the village as I ran around with the boys of my age. I had a shock of my life one day when we strayed too close to the Fon's palace, the seat of the traditional authority of the village and one of the boys I was with invited me to go in with him. Even in Nkar, I had never ventured within a mile of our Fon's palace that was located down the valley from the parish. I dreaded those places for I had a deadly fear of masquerades (jujus). The image of such places in my mind was always that of people tearing the mouths of fowls and twisting the necks of goats and spilling blood all around, a totally unchristian practice that could land the practitioners in hell, if they were to die without first confessing such abominable acts to the priest.

Even though I was hundreds of miles away from Pa Mathias' immediate supervision, I still could not muster the courage to go into the Tabenken palace. My friends even invited me to go with them into the inner sanctum where the masquerades were kept. They told me those masquerades were hanging on the walls and ceiling while some were stashed at a corner of the "juju" house. One day, one of them even asked his father in my presence to take the two of us with him into the inner corners of the palace so I could see the masquerades and, amazingly enough, the old man agreed. I took to my heels and never stopped till I reached home. From that day, and until I left the village, I never went near their palace again.

There was a Nso woman married in the village, who stepped up to cook for us. All I needed to do was go to her house in the evening and the food would be ready. She lived barely a hundred yards from our house. Soon my brother and I became like members of her family, especially when she heard that our mother was originally from Meluf village, which was where she too came from. When my brother told her the name of my mother's compound, she nearly broke down in tears. "We are the same blood," she said, wiping tears from her eyes. Then she mentioned the names of people whom Lawrence recognised as our maternal relatives. From then on, Lawrence began to send me with a steady supply of vegetables and meat for her family, which she deeply appreciated. Her husband, a village elder, was also very welcoming and would often bring us litres of sweet palm wine, which I really adored.

Later that year, we moved closer to the school and the church. We took rooms in a house that had originally been built like a dormitory to accommodate primary school pupils from distant outstations, who could not travel between their own villages and the parish school on a daily basis. That was before the parish opened schools in those outstations. That building then stood empty until a teacher came from outside the village, like us. Next door, lived the Fondong family. Mr.

Michael Fondong was from Bali Nyonga, after Bamenda. He was the school headmaster. He was a tall, lanky, calm gentleman; a father of two, Bernard and a girl, Edith, who we referred to as 'E'. Mrs. Theresia Fondong was very motherly to me and she was also a great cook. She literally took over our feeding, especially when my brother left to participate in the marking of the First School Leaving Certificate examination in faraway Mankon town in Bamenda. I still visited the Nso family that had fed us prior to our moving to the new location and the kids came to see me just about each morning when they left their doctrine classes at the parish, which was just nearby. From time to time, their mother, a precious soul, would send us some food, or fresh groundnuts and corn, and Lawrence never failed to send me to her with bottles of oil, some meat and rice, which she greatly appreciated. There was everything to make us feel part of the community, and life was good.

***

The parish priest was another Dutchman whose name I forget. Unlike Fara Nji, he was very much a gentleman. He took a liking for me from the moment he heard I had been an altar boy in Nkar. I remember him telling some schoolboys of the village: "Make wuna see dis small pikin fine-fine. Na mass boy already. Wuna dey here big, big boys dem with bia-bia for mop, wuna no fit recite one smol prayer, one smol prayer dasso, for Mass." He did not hide his admiration for Nsoland which he said God had blessed and endowed with rulers who had had the wisdom to fully embrace Catholicism. He would tell the others, "Wuna for dis kontri, wuna no get sense no smol; wuna say na Baptist church wuna like. Weti Baptist church don bring wuna. Make wuna go for Banso see big, big church and big, big waapita wey Catholic church don build for dey. Wuna na foolish people for dis kontri."

He had apparently served for a while as curate of a parish in Nsoland before being assigned to the Tabenken parish and he said Nso boys were much more likely to go to the seminary than the Tabenken boys. For that reason, he assigned me a number of tasks in the sacristy – arranging vestments properly in the cloisters, pouring out ashes from the thurible after benediction on Sundays and seeing to the general cleanness of the sacristy, a task I did with much delight and pride. At the end of the year, as I was preparing to leave for good, he surprised me by summoning me to his house, thanking me for my services to the church, and giving me some money. When I showed my brother the money, he expressed surprise that the priest had decided to show such appreciation for my assistance at the sacristy. He then told me to use it as I pleased. My friends and I went to a nearby shop and bought all the sweets, candies and groundnuts the money could give us.

The parish priest would often point to the Baptist mission perched on a hill at a distance and tell the young altar boys that anyone who was not willing to come to church could cross over there. I was quick to learn that between the Baptists and the Catholics in the village, there was a long-standing feud. Things were made worse because the Baptist school had a senior football team that regularly thrashed our own team, and even teams outside Tabenken. Their players controlled the ball admirably well and they had strikers who drove the ball home with unforgiving accuracy. Their goalkeeper, who was rumoured to be a Muslim masquerading as a Baptist, would spring up like a tiger and bring the ball down with unbelievable dexterity. Rumours were rife in Catholic circles that the Baptists were winning those matches through the use of charms that they received from their Fulani neighbours. What type of church was that, many Catholics wondered, that would shamelessly resort to black magic? Should it not, like the Catholic church, fight to eliminate magical practices from the surface of the earth? But there it was, promoting it instead. Could that really be said to be a church of God? Those are some of the questions that floated in the air in Catholic circles in the village.

However, if the truth were to be told, any fair-minded person would have admitted that the Baptists had superior athletes in every sporting domain. Even the girls' netball team thrashed ours mercilessly during regional competitions organised from Binju, the administrative headquarters, and involving teams in the whole division. It was not rare for the Baptist athletes to travel as far away as Bamenda and come back brandishing trophies that made the mouths of even their worst enemy – the Catholics – water abundantly.

*　*　*

On the whole, I enjoyed my one-year stay in Tabenken. Whenever I went to the market, the women would all cheerfully greet me as *mooh Chia* (the teacher's son). Before the year was out, I was already expressing myself pretty fluently in Limbum, the local language.

Come holiday time, we would go back home to Nkar. My brother knew people who could arrange for a taxi or a private car to pick us up from our house directly to Ndu, which had a big market and a motor park from where we would get easy transportation to Kumbo, and then to Nkar less than ten miles away. Tabenken lies in a valley and is rimmed on all sides by hills that seemed to discourage frequent visits from taxis. I remember once being given a ride directly from Tabenken to Kumbo by the parish priest himself. My brother had asked him to kindly drop me at Squares in Kumbo from where I could easily catch a ride home. He had graciously agreed to take me along in what turned out to be the most silent and solemn ride anyone ever gave me. He practically never said a word to me and I never volunteered any. Even if I had wanted to speak, I would not have known what to say. But it was a pleasant ride, all the same, with me sitting in the back seat all alone, avoiding to look in the mirror for fear our eyes might cross. I just relaxed and enjoyed the beauty of the scenery, the hills that seemed to roll and twist and turn on and on as they rushed to the distant horizon. Years later, I would learn that beyond those hills lay another country, Nigeria, where my father had travelled as a young man, selling kolanuts to the Hausas of the north, and mastering the language with admirable ease. I remember him saying that their road to Nigeria passed through Mbumland before crossing to Nigeria.

As we drove by, I admired the farms, all green with maize and fresh groundnuts and fresh potatoes. Then we were in the village of Tatum with beautiful buildings perched on a hill, housing a Catholic teacher training college with a well-established reputation for churning out well-groomed teachers, who gave Catholic education the high reputation it enjoyed throughout West Cameroon. Those were days before the government stepped in to seize some confessional schools (Catholic, Baptist and Presbyterian), turning them to government schools with the hardly convincing excuse that it wanted to make primary education free and more accessible to ordinary Cameroonian children. Lofty though that may sound, the seized schools did eventually lose the sheen and lustre of the days when they were under missionary control, especially their reputation for bringing up well-disciplined children. With time, government schools became synonymous with laxity both on the side of teachers as of the children they were teaching.

As we made our descent to Kumbo town, we saw to our right an impressive hospital, the Banso Baptist Hospital, that belonged to the Baptist mission, of all people. Those were the people who, according to our parish priest, had nothing that could remotely rival anything owned by the Catholic church. I wondered what might have been going through his mind when we drove past such outstanding structures built by those he said were incapable of matching the Catholics in any way. A little further down, we drove past the Presbyterian bookshop, the only one in town worth the name. Catholics could not boast of a similar bookshop, as far as I knew. Then there was the Presbyterian Church which, it was true, could not compare with the massive Catholic Church nearby but which was no less beautifully built.

The parish priest dropped me off around Squares in Kumbo. I thanked him and he merely nodded his head. I took my bag and boarded a taxi for Nkar, ten miles away. Once back in Nkar, I walked around with the inflated ego of someone who had just come back from outside the village. I was, however, very aware that coming from Nkambe could in no way be compared to coming from Bamenda or down south – Victoria, Buea, Kumba, Mamfe. Those were places where everyone was said to roll in wealth and where all kinds of goodies were within everyone's reach. Was it not down south that white people were said to drive expensive cars and share sweets to whoever happened to come their way, especially kids? What was there in Nkambe for anyone to boast of? That was the question my friend, Dominic, asked, pouting his lips and hissing a sound of disdain when we met outside the church one Sunday. That disdainful reaction came after I had proudly briefed those of them who had crowded around me after Mass on my stay in Tabenken.

"What of you?" I asked, fury oiling my voice as his reaction stung my ego like a bee. "Have you ever been even to Kumbo, just up here? Or even to Jakiri next door? And you dare question me for having gone to Tabenken. Don't you know that from Tabenken we often travel to Nkambe, which is a big town with an agricultural farm with many animals from where we buy milk and butter? It also has a police station and a big hospital. Have you seen any such place in your life?" For an answer, he turned to one of our friends, Aloysius, and asked "Did I not just come back from Bamenda the other day after spending a week with my aunty who lives there?" No one seemed to remember and we all started drifting away to our various homes leaving him standing there alone. In fact, I could not say that I was not happy to have scored a solid point against a rival, who always claimed to know everything. I knew he would think twice before contradicting me again. For a day or two, he refused to say a word to me even though we met just about every day at the parish where we kicked a cloth-wrapped ball we had made ourselves out of old clothes. Before long, however, peace returned to the group and he and I became friends again.

CHAPTER 3

BINJU, NKAMBE - 1964

The following year when I was moving to the final class, Standard Six, my brother, Lawrence, was transferred to the divisional capital, Nkambe town, some ten miles north of Tabenken village. We had visited Nkambe during a number of events such as the National Youth Day and other Catholic feasts that brought Catholic schools together. Lawrence was to assist the headmaster of the Catholic School that was located in Binju, a neighbourhood which served as the administrative seat of the division where the district office and other government outfits were found. There was also a police station nearby and one of our closest neighbours was a young police officer, who worked in communication using the Morse code. He was a proud young man who took delight in explaining to me how he sent messages through frequent beeps on a machine to Bamenda, Buea and even London. He was gracious enough to invite me to his office to watch him in action. I was so delighted with what he showed me that for some time I dreamed of joining the police force just to learn to send messages through the Morse code machine. He, however, seemed to have a weakness for women and that bothered my brother a great deal.

There was a day he saw a girl across the road a distance away and sent me to tell her to come to him. The girl did and the man literally locked her up in his room for two days running, and the girl only succeeded to leave through the bathroom window that had no iron protectors. That caused a scandal in the village and when questioned why she had come to the man in the first place, she said I had invited her to come. Mercifully, no one believed her and my brother confronted the policeman and the encounter was not a pleasant one. The man merely shrugged it off with a smile, saying that my brother was making a fuss for nothing and that he should stop shielding me from the realities of the world and start teaching me the marvels of life. There was nothing more marvellous than resting in the arms of a well-endowed woman at the end of a long, tiring day, he said and my brother nearly hit the ceiling with rage. He then told my brother to grow up and stop whining like an old woman. Lawrence did not find what he said funny at all, and never forgave him for such effrontery.

One day, he asked me how old I was. I told him I was 13 soon to be 14. He nodded his head and then surprised, even frightened me, by asking if I had a girlfriend. "No!" I said in fright, utterly taken aback by his question. Even though I was in class with girls, even sharing a desk with one, my usual shyness would not let me even think of asking any of them to be my girlfriend. Never!

"You're old enough to have a girlfriend," he said, scanning my astonished face with a glee on his. "I first slept with a girl at your age. But will your idiot of a brother let you explore the world, know what real life is, and what is real life without women?" I was so astonished I ran away. But then something had been planted in my mind. What of the catechist's daughter, who had stood behind me at a choir practice the other day and pressed her full-fledged chest against my back? Was that deliberate or accidental? Sensations I never even knew existed had shot through my whole body and I felt really uneasy long thereafter. I avoided eye contact with her merely because I did not know how else to react towards her. She was a beautiful girl but I did not know how to approach her or tell her I liked her. Even if I had said it and she said, "Yes, let's be friends!" what next would I tell her? Run back to our neighbour and ask him for advice? Confusion ran amok in my mind!

We were, however, saved from further embarrassment when the

landlord heard of the scandal with the young girl, who happened to be his niece, and threw out the turbulent tenant. But I liked him, not so much for his womanising side, which I then knew nothing about, although he was trying to wrap me in it, but more because he was a very knowledgeable man. He loved to discuss politics and analyse historical events in detail. His radio was perpetually tuned to the BBC shortwave band and he would keep it going at full blast during the six o'clock evening news from Bush House in London. It was from him that I heard the name 'Bush House' and I remember asking him why such a name to a place in London, of all places. I do not remember what explanation he gave, but he always seemed to have an explanation for everything. He would call me to come over and listen to the BBC.

"That's the great voice of Ian Stamp for you, my friend," he would exclaim and then repeat after the broadcaster, deepening his voice as he imitated the Englishman. Then he would shake his head and say, "That's British English for you, my friend; that's what English should sound like. Not this bush English you hear these fellows speaking from Buea and Yaounde. No, that's no English at all! That's even worse than Pidgin! Have you ever seen me listening to them? No, I never do. Am I mad?"

He seemed to bear a special grudge against the Honourable John Ngu Foncha, who was then the Prime Minister of West Cameroon. He said Foncha was from his village and he could not wait to challenge that son-of-a-nobody and send him packing from the Prime Minister's Lodge in Buea.

"I am the only one from my constituency that Foncha is really scared of; you can ask him. He knows that if free and fair elections were conducted today, I would roll him in the dust."

What a consummate entertainer he was and I was somewhat sad to see him go, although I could not say it to my brother's hearing, especially not the girlfriend issue. To him, that good-for-nothing fellow's expulsion was good riddance. I never saw him again.

* * *

Binju also hosted some economic activity, especially the government agricultural farm with well aligned rows of vegetable beds that always looked green with carrots, red and yellow pepper, garden eggs, among others. There was also a fishpond from where big fish was harvested from time to time for sale. We would gather around the pond as it was being drained to reveal fish of various sizes and we would watch keenly as the catchers selected which ones to harvest and which ones to let go. We would giggle as they chased the fish and try to subdue them although some would often slip out of their hands and rush to hide under the rocks. Then when the harvesting was over, the pond would again be refilled with fresh water and the fish that had been left behind would again emerge from their hideouts and swim joyfully around the pond. There were also cows, many with short horns, very much unlike the Fulani cows we were used to seeing with huge horns that pointed to the skies. Sheep and goats also grazed leisurely on the vast expanse of land around the village. The agricultural centre produced fresh milk and butter which my brother bought on a regular basis and which we all consumed with immense delight.

I continued to serve as an altar boy at the Catholic church in Binju. There was no Catholic church or school in Nkambe town itself, nor was there any in the neighbouring villages, which seemed to have been lost to Protestantism. Islam also had a strong foothold around the Nkambe main market. There was a mosque in which adherents prayed by knocking their heads on the ground facing the east, where, we were told, their own 'Vatican' called 'Mecca' was located. In the morning and in the evening, you would hear the high-pitched voice of the imam summoning devotees to prayer. There was also a thriving and vibrant Baptist community that quickly gained notoriety for their long processions to the market on market days. They were accompanied by much drumming and dancing with pastors preaching from makeshift pulpits all day long. That was the first time I saw a church other than Catholic at close quarters.

In my village Nkar, you were either from a Catholic home, or a non-Catholic home, which we disdainfully referred to as 'pagan homes'. My family also had family members who attended what we called the "Hausa church", meaning the Mosque. To us, the Hausa of northern Nigeria were synonymous with Islam and anyone who was converted to Islam automatically earned the name 'wir gassa', the Lamnso word for Hausa man or woman. Muslims were mainly found in the neighbouring village of Jakiri, where Islam had found particularly rich soil in which to sink its roots.

The story goes that up until quite recently, the only known inhabitants of Jakiri were a Fulani pastoralist, called Jajiri, and his family. He was said to have come from where no one knew to rear his cattle on the nearby hills and valleys where they could roam far and wide. The only contact he seemed to have had with the local farming communities around was when his children came to buy things from the provisions stores nearby and his wives sold butter and milk, which they called "nono" or "kwasham". The only customers they seemed to have were schoolteachers, the only people who could afford to spend money on such luxuries as milk and butter, which were beyond the reach of ordinary villagers.

I recall a cousin of mine dismissing teachers as lazy people who spent their time sitting around and toying with chalk all day long and then going home to drink milk and climb on their women. He said teachers had hands that were softer than a baby's behind. What sort of people were those? The hands of real men had to be as hard and rough as his from back-breaking work in farms, he would say, showing you his coarse hands that felt like a rock.

As time passed, some people from distant villages came to settle around Jajiri's huts and began to encroach on his land with their farms. The poor Fulani man, who spoke Lamnso with a funny accent, packed his bags and led his family further up into the hills where grass grew in abundance and where his cattle had open land on which to graze in peace. The settlers reportedly deformed his name to Jakiri, which they gave to their new settlement. The inhabitants of the surrounding villages had always known the place, prior to Jajiri's arrival, as "Kifee".

Not long thereafter, some Hausa people, tracing their origins to the Islamic Caliphates of Northern Nigeria, came in too, settling there and quickly making religious inroads into what had hitherto been the exclusive domain of traditional religious practitioners. Unlike Christianity, which frowned on certain traditional practices, notably polygamy, Islam fully embraced polygamy and, before long, drew into their fold quite a sizeable following.

* * *

The daughter of my father's immediate sister became the wife of a Muslim, one of the early converts to Islam who had settled in the neighbouring village of Ber, a few miles from Jakiri. Although my father spoke the Hausa language very well, having travelled in his younger years to Yola, Sokoto and Kaduna in Northern Nigeria in the company of kolanut traders, he did not have anything good to say about their religion. Whenever his sister's children came for a visit, which was often, he would hold long conversations with them in Hausa, a language he mastered well. He spoke it better than many of the Nso converts to Islam. In fact, towards the end of his earthly journey, my father spent his days in front of his house, when the sun was up, or near a bonfire in his kitchen, always with a transistor radio by his side. It was tuned to one station only, Radio Kaduna. If anyone dared to move the dial to another station, he would scream and grumble for days on end. He often set it to the highest volume possible and we would see him nodding his head and often bursting into laughter as the speakers carried out discussions on whatever the topic was. We thus became familiar with Islam in our home through our aunt.

It was said that other churches had been refused a spot in Nkar village when the then ruling Fon threw in his lot with Catholicism. When other proselytes came around, they were kindly urged to head further north to places like Kumbo, the region's chief town, the seat of the Nso Fondom, where the paramount ruler of the land had his palace. It was said that Kumbo could accommodate anyone and anything. After all, the argument went, it was home to the largest weekly market that opened its doors even to the worst forms of individuals from around the world. What with those bad boys, commonly called "bambeh boys", who skipped school, smoked 'banga', roamed the streets, and stole from peace-loving people? One of those bad boys even snatched a loincloth off a woman's waist in broad daylight, thus exposing the poor woman's nudity to the universe. That could only happen in Kumbo, not in our peace-loving Nkar, the locals would say. And what of those girls who shamelessly opened their legs for a fee to anyone who happened to pass by? To Nkar villagers, Kumbo was a place to visit sparingly, mainly on market days, and then rush out before those women of light virtue emptied the unsuspecting victim's pockets. Stories abounded of villagers who would carry heavy calabashes of palm-wine on their heads from faraway places like Mensai down the valley, to Kumbo. The women to whom they sold the palm-wine would entice them to spend the money they had just earned to buy and drink the same palm-wine they had just sold. Many would stumble back home in the night drunk and more broke than they were before.

It was in Nkambe that I came to know that there were churches, like the Baptists, that allowed their members to dance during service. On market days, they would dance from the church to the market square, with their women kicking their legs in the air. That was an astonishing spectacle to me and I wondered what would happen if the scanty loincloths some of them wrapped around their waist came loose and dropped on the ground. Would people not be forced to see what was not meant to be seen in broad daylight? How shameful that would be! To my Catholic mind, nothing could be more revolting.

There was no drum playing, dancing or noisy singing in the Catholic church then, and to us, that was how a true church had to be. We had been told in our doctrine classes that there was no possibility of salvation outside the Catholic church; so, it was really strange for me to see people singing and dancing in the market square in the name of

Jesus Christ. Were they not openly committing a sin by calling God's name in vain? My Catholic mind told me they were better off joining the Muslims and heading straight for perdition.

***

It was in Binju that I wrote the common entrance examination into secondary school. Before the government-sponsored common entrance examination could hold, our parish priest announced that he would be conducting a test in religious knowledge and only those boys who would like to attend the Bishop Rogan Minor Seminary in Soppo, Buea, with the possibility of heading for the priesthood, would be allowed to write it.

I was among the first boys to sign up for the test and when the results were released a few days later, two of us were shortlisted for an interview with a priest who would be coming from outside. It turned out to be the Rector of the Minor Seminary in Buea himself.

We were called up for the interview. When I gave my name, he asked if I had heard of Bishop Rogan College before. I said I had not and for a moment I thought he might ask me to leave but he did not. He said the parish priest had said some good things about me, especially that I was a good altar boy and that my test results were there to prove that I was a serious candidate for his school. That compliment felt good and I remember smiling timidly and staring at my toes in the process. He also said I was expressing myself well in good English and he hoped I would be a good student when I came to Bishop Rogan College, which he called BIROCOL. He was indirectly telling me that he thought I was good material for his college and eventually for the priesthood.

A strange thing then happened. I noticed that as he talked, he began to lean to one side of his seat and before I knew it he let out a loud fart that took me completely by surprise. I had not then known that anyone could feel free to fart so openly, not only once but twice, the second one sounding even much louder than the first. I quickly looked away, avoiding to look at him for fear our eyes might meet. But he did not seem in the least worried as he kept his eyes glued to his notebook. In Nsoland, farting so openly was simply unthinkable. Even when an elder happened to mess the air in the presence of a kid, the said elder would start shouting and accusing the kid who would be lucky if he or she was not chased out with a slap to the head. But there I was, in the presence of a white man to boot, an elder too, who had so shamelessly and openly farted in the presence of a child. That was something!

"Ok, Martin. See you in Buea next July," he said as he shook my astonished hand.

"You will be hearing from us through your parish priest. Goodbye and call in the next candidate, please." I thanked him and left the room.

I asked my friend to go in and then waited impatiently for him to come out. I could not wait to tell him what had just happened. As soon as he came out, I did not even ask if he too had been admitted. All I thought about was the man's fart.

"Did he also fart in your presence?" I asked as soon as he stepped out the door.

My friend stopped in his tracks and looked at me as if I had just gone mad.

"I mean the priest, did he also fart in your presence?" Then I told him what had just happened.

"No, he didn't and I am beginning to think that something is not right in that head of yours! Where did you get that type of crazy idea from?" he asked, looking at me in a funny way.

"No, it's true; he farted, not once but twice!" I sounded hurt that he did not believe me.

"You don't mean it. I've never heard that white people also fart. Even if they do, I don't believe a white priest would fart in the presence of a young child like you? Are you sure you really heard it?"

"Oh yes, I heard it with my own two ears, and I even thought you heard it too since it really sounded loud. It was not only once, but twice; the second time sounding really loud."

"What? Two times?" he asked pointing two fingers at me.

"Yes, two times!" I screamed. "I could've sworn you also heard it from where you were sitting!"

"I heard nothing. Why did he not fart when I was with him? He only chose to do it when you were there. Those rabbit ears of yours will hear what no one should ever hear."

"I don't know why he didn't do it in your presence! Maybe he didn't just feel like it when you were there. But all I know is that he did it, not once but twice, believe me!"

"I don't believe you. I still don't even believe that white people also fart as we do. We mess the air all the time because of the bad food we eat. Do you think they eat the same type of food we eat? My uncle is the parish priest's cook and he tells us what they eat and what they don't eat. Do you know how often my uncle goes to the agric farm to buy fresh vegetables and eggs and meat? Almost everyday. Do you think someone who eats that type of food can have gas in his stomach? Just walk by the window of the kitchen in the Father's house and smell the sweet aroma from his kitchen. No, I don't believe they fart as we do. We pass gas constantly because of all the bad food we eat; all the foo-foo corn and njama-njama and beans and cabbage. Cabbage! Yaak! I hate cabbage! When you eat the type of things we eat, you're forced to fart. And by the way, don't forget that you're talking about a priest. Saying such a thing about a priest is definitely a mortal sin. You remember the lesson the parish priest taught us about the different sins: venial sin and mortal sin. What you are saying now is definitely a mortal sin and don't forget that if you die now and you have such thoughts in your mind, Satan will only be too happy to welcome you in his kingdom. And don't say that I never warned you."

"I know what I heard," I said, anger rising in my throat. How could that fellow not believe me?

When my friend saw that I was not backing down, he came close to me, one of his fingers pushing me on the forehead, "don't also forget that there are some sins that only the bishop can forgive, and what you're saying about a priest is one of them. And how many times does the bishop come here? For the time you have been here, have you seen him come for a visit? And what if you have to wait for him before you confess a sin, and you happen to die before he comes, what happens to your soul? Have you thought about that?"

When he mentioned the bishop, memories of my Confirmation came flashing back to mind. I wondered how anyone could ever muster the courage to confess one's sins to that colossus of a man. But then I could not remember our parish priest saying that if you said something about another person you must confess to the bishop. He was warning us against backbiting, "kongossa," which he said was spreading among us in school. The only time I heard him mention the bishop's name was when he talked to some girls and warned them if they were ever to kill a baby in their womb, they would have to confess their sin to the bishop. I was not even sure how a girl could kill a child in her womb, and, in the first place, I was not a girl; so why should I have to go to confess to the bishop simply for saying what I heard? I heard it, not once but twice! What my friend was saying did not make sense at all.

"Come-on," I said. "You're blowing this thing out of all proportion. How can what I have said be considered a mortal sin, or even a simple venial sin since that's what I heard?"

"Just say one word about it in front of the others," he warned, "and you will be in for it. Remember that when we go back to class, they will certainly be curious to know how the interview went, and just whisper what you've just said to me to anyone else and the whole school will hear of it and the parish priest will hear of it too. Imagine what he will say if he hears that you're going around telling the whole school that the priest, who came from Buea, farted in your presence. You will be in some serious trouble, mind you. I have spoken my mind. Do as you like, but don't say I didn't warn you. And by the way, you and I have been admitted into the minor seminary and even before you get there you're already spreading lies about their priest. Go ahead, sing it from the treetops and the rooftops of the village, if you want. That is your problem." With that, he walked away without even as much as a glance behind to see if I was following him. I then decided to walk back home instead of following him to class.

Later that evening, I told my brother about the interview and he was happy to hear that I had been granted admission into BIRO-COL. He said I was making him proud and that we would see what the test into the government college in Victoria would look like. He then added that even if that one did not turn out well, I already had this one firmly under my belt. I did not, however, make any mention of the priest letting out gas in my presence; nor did anyone else hear about it in school. And the case was thus closed.

***

The date for the entrance examination into the other secondary schools was fast approaching. It was strange that it was only on the eve of the test that I heard of a school called the Federal Bilingual Grammar School that was said to be located in Victoria, far down the coast. Information about such far-flung schools was not easy to come by, especially as the Federal Bilingual Grammar School was still in its infancy. There were far away giants that were known all over West Cameroon; schools that had long established a solid reputation for academic excellence such as Saint Joseph's College, Sasse, Cameroon Protestant College, Bali, Sacred Heart College, Mankon, Queen of the Holy Rosary College, Okoyong in Mamfe for girls. If one had to go that far, better go to one of them, not to a new school no one had ever heard of.

There were nearby schools still in their infancy, Saint Augustine's College in Kumbo (Catholic) and Joseph Merrick College in Ndu (Baptist), for example, which had the advantage of proximity to home. They too were beginning to edge their way into the discussions of many potential candidates. But a brand-new school, like the Federal Bilingual Grammar School, lost in the thick forests of Victoria, was not likely to attract many candidates, even though it was said to be government-owned with all tuition paid. The immediate picture that came to mind when anyone talked about Victoria was of stifling heat, omnipresent malaria-distributing mosquitoes, the ever-present stench of rotting fish and cramped houses with people said to be defecating in the open. Who could ever think of going to study in such a place? Who wanted to send their children to a school with those French fellows who were said to be so prone to violence, anyway? The stakes were high against the new school in distant Victoria.

Few of us therefore paid any attention when someone from the Delegation of Education came to sensitise potential candidates to try their luck by taking the entrance examination into that relatively new school, fully government-sponsored, called the Federal Bilingual Grammar School, where children were brought together in one place from all the corners of Cameroon. He, however, warned that the selection was very rigorous and that only a few of those who wrote the test were ever selected. It was an all-boys boarding school, he said before adding that he hoped we would take advantage of the singular opportunity to be among the select few. Like the rest of my friends, I merely shrugged it off; after all, did I not already have a spot firmly secure in the minor seminary in Buea? So, why worry?

My brother, Lawrence, would not hear of it. He took the admission form from the delegation official and completed it himself on the spot and had me sign it. He then gave it back to the official, who congratulated him on a wise choice that could give his brother a big boost in his life. He left with one or two other forms, expressing regret that few people in the region seemed to show any interest simply because they did not know what they were depriving their children of.

On the test day, I was the only one from my school to write the test to the Federal Bilingual Grammar School. A handful of other candidates for the same school were from the other primary schools in Nkambe. The other classmates of mine present were writing for admission into other schools. That was the second test I was writing in about three weeks; the other being the religion test which the parish priest set and graded himself. The fact that only two of us were finally shortlisted and interviewed by an outside priest, the Rector of a minor seminary in person, spoke volumes to me. It simply said to me: "Man, you can do it!" That is why I approached the second test with the same determination as the first one and I was surprised by how simple the questions were, be they in arithmetic, history, geography or English. Students were given a choice of three essay topics. At one stage, I looked up and saw fear in the eyes of one candidate who seemed to be literally trembling with fright. He kept looking around as if seeking for help. Then he made as if to stand up, but instead leaned over the shoulder of the candidate in front of him. Unfortunately for him, an examiner caught him in the act, rushed out to notify her boss, who came in and ordered the candidate to leave the room immediately. The fellow cried and begged that he had done nothing wrong. The chief supervisor was not impressed and asked him to leave immediately or else he would not be allowed to write any other test into any secondary school in the country. We could hear the poor fellow sobbing as he walked away. The other candidates then knew a similar fate awaited them, if they too were caught cheating. The ever-vigilant examiners seemed to have their eyes on each candidate at once and we all breathed a sigh of relief when the test ended with no other candidate being shown the door.

During the test, I banished all fear from my heart, telling myself that with a firm admission into another school already warm in my pocket, I had nothing to lose in the second test. The whines and whimpers and lengthy sighs I heard from other candidates had no effect on me. I completed the test well ahead of the scheduled time and had sufficient time to review my English essay. It took slightly over a month for the results to be released.

We would probably never have heard of the results had it not been for a happy coincidence. My brother called it a 'God incidence.' There was a well-known mail service called 'Mail Van' that ran between Bamenda and Nkambe twice or three times a week. It collected mail from the main post office in Bamenda for the different post offices along the Bamenda-Nkambe stretch of the Ring Road. On its return journey, it retrieved mail from the same post offices for the main mail sorting and distribution centre in Mankon town. The contract was awarded to a well-known and successful businessman, Sylvester Kindzeka Kilo of Sop village about three miles from our village of Nkar. The man in charge, Ben Shang, whom I always referred to as 'Uncle Ben', was a friend of my brother's. It was not rare for him to drop by our house for a drink or a meal when he was in town.

Late one evening, we heard a knock on our door. We had already gone to bed for the night. I heard my brother asking who it was but I did not hear the answer clearly. Then I heard him strike a match to light the kerosene lamp in his room. He came out of his room with the lamp in hand and opened the door. It was then that I recognised Uncle Ben's voice apologising for dropping by so late. My brother said it was okay and invited him to come in and take a seat. He said he was in a hurry and would not come in. He said he had a letter for me from the Delegation of Education in Bamenda. He had gone there to collect mail for their office in Nkambe at the time the interview-invitation slips into the Federal Bilingual Grammar School were being prepared. There was only one for Nkambe and he was happy to see that it was for me. He was therefore the bearer of good news for me. When I heard what he was saying, I stood up from bed, came out and greeted him. He congratulated me on my success and said he had been told that few candidates succeeded to get admission into that school. I thanked him for bringing the admission slip to us.

My brother opened the envelope and, lo and behold, it bore a congratulatory note about my success in the written test. I was therefore being invited for the interview scheduled for Saturday at Sacred Heart College in Mankon town. That was just two days away, as it was on Thursday! My brother said it was too close and wondered what to do.

"Listen," Uncle Ben said, "I am going back to Bamenda tomorrow. You two can come along and your problem is solved." He was a God-sent messenger and my brother told him we would be ready for him in the morning. We quickly put the few clothes we were to take along in one bag and were ready and waiting when the mail van hooted its horn in front of our house at 6:30 the next morning, and we were off.

The mail van made several stops along the way, collecting mail from designated spots for the main post office in Bamenda. It was amazing to see what great service that van rendered the people in the various villages of the region and I came to have great respect for their work. Uncle Ben and the driver were showered with warm accolades along the way. They seemed to know everyone we met and people rushed out of their homes to greet them or thank them for bringing their letters and parcels, or for collecting those they were sending out and ensuring that they reached the right destination. It was an impressive operation and I was glad my brother was on friendly terms with Uncle Ben. Had that not been the case, we might never have received the interview-invitation slip, or it might have come too late to be of use to anyone.

＊＊

We dropped off in Bambui and bade Uncle Ben and the driver goodbye. Uncle Ben simply told me, "Martin, I know you to be a smart boy. So, bring back good news. That's all I'm waiting for." I assured him I would do my best and they drove off. We walked about a quarter mile to the home of Lawrence's friend, himself a teacher at the Catholic Teacher Training College that prepared candidates for the Grade Three Teacher Certificate. Lawrence had also graduated from that college years previously. His friend and wife warmly welcomed us and congratulated me on my success in the highly competitive test into what he called 'a unique school in the country.' Lawrence had to remind them that I was still going for the interview and that the trophy was not yet in the bag. It all depended on me and on what I do the next day. They all said they were confident I would do well.

"If he takes after you, Larry, and just by looking at him I can see that he does," said our host, "then there will be nothing to be afraid of." Other friends, who had come in when they heard my brother was around, also congratulated me and said if I was as sharp as my brother had always been, then they were sure I would do well. Lawrence said he felt humbled by their compliments and thanked them for it. They all said: "Na today we know you, oga? Sense full-up for your head! Sense pass king!" They all laughed as they exchanged memories of times spent together in different teacher training colleges, some of them having also graduated, like Lawrence, from the same school they were then teaching in. Our host then took some time to give me a few useful tips to use when answering interviewer questions.

"You have to speak the truth and nothing but the truth."

"So help me God," another friend chimed in, and we all laughed.

"Yes, the truth," continued our host. "If you lie and try to trick the interviewers, they will know and you will fail. If you don't know an answer to a question, it will be better to say you don't know than to give a dumb answer out of fear, or try to cheat with a fake answer. They will know and they will read through you like a book," he said amidst much laughter from the others. They then took turns to recall the interviews they themselves had conducted in the course of their career; how some candidates would fake an American accent and sound really phony; others would be completely tongue-tight and it would take tact on the interviewer's part to help them loosen their tongue. And sometimes when they did, an excellent candidate would emerge, one whom an impatient interviewer might have tossed aside as not good material for their school.

We had a good night's rest and a hefty breakfast in the morning from our host's wife, a shy-looking, self-effacing woman, who looked more like the host's first daughter than his wife. Their two young kids, who were already in bed when we arrived, looked at me with visible curiosity. They put down their heads shyly when their mother asked them to greet us and when I stretched out my hand, they both shook it lightly without raising their eyes, the little boy sucking on his thumb. We said goodbye to them and went out into the cold, refreshing morning air. Lawrence's friend pulled out his car, a Renault 4, from the garage and we rode together to Sacred Heart College, the site of the interview. He reminded me not to forget the tips he had given me the day before. I said "Thank you very much, uncle. I will remember them." He wished me luck and before leaving he reminded Lawrence, who had told him we intended to go up to Nkar immediately after the interview, that if we decided not to go up, the door to his house was always open and that our bed was still warm. We thanked him and watched him reverse his car and disappear out the college gate.

Other candidates were there already; those from the same school were standing in small groups with some of their teachers present and keeping watch over them. Some came alone or with their parents or guardians. My brother recognised some of the teachers and parents and they exchanged greetings, each saying how it was necessary to follow their wards for the interview and give them the support they needed. One man said he would be rushing to Our Lady of Lourdes College shortly after that as his daughter was being interviewed for that school. "We go do how na, papa? You bonam, you get for lookot-am. You get for run after dem till they comot for you hand for good. Na dat time you fit relax drink your one smol shomer! We go do how?"

They all laughed and the kids standing a few feet away also smiled and I knew that those men were indirectly lowering the stress of those of us to be interviewed. My brother then saw another teacher of the school going into one classroom. He called out his name and walked to him. They greeted each other warmly, exchanged a few pleasantries and then my brother asked about the interview rooms, since it was getting to 9 o'clock, my interview hour. He took us to the information board where he ran his finger on the lists posted there and then said, "Yes, the Federal Bilingual Grammar School is on the first floor. Take this stairway, young man and it should lead you there, Room 3." He said since my brother's presence would not be needed up there, he could come with him to his office, an invitation my brother happily accepted. It was clear they had known each other for long. There was no one on the first floor and I looked for Room 3. It was open and someone saw me from inside and beckoned me to come in.

"Are you here for the interview into the Federal Bilingual Grammar School, my son?"

I said, "Yes, Sir, I am."

"You're in the right place, come in and take a seat." I thanked him and sat across the table from him. He was neatly dressed in a long-sleeve shirt and had a blue tie over grey trousers. Two other gentlemen were at an adjacent table and I also greeted them. They responded warmly and one of them, who had a coat on but no tie, asked me for my invitation slip, which I gave him. He then asked me where I came from. When I said Nkambe he said that was a long way off and asked if I had just come from there that morning. I said no, that my brother and I came the day before, spent a night in Bambui and came into town that morning.

The third gentleman, who was fairly elderly then asked if I was Kenjo Jumbam's brother. The answer being affirmative, he said he knew my brother well and that he was a writer. Then he asked me, "Are you a writer too?" His question caught me by surprise and I said, "No, Sir! I am still in primary school!" They all laughed and said even primary school children these days were already writing novels. Another said they were writing more love letters to their girlfriends than novels. Once more, they laughed and I smiled shyly, not knowing whether to laugh too or to just look away. I was in the presence of elders and I did not know whether it was appropriate for me to share in their jokes. So, I preferred to be quiet.

When they talked of my brother's writings, I remembered some books in history and geography he wrote that we were using in class. He also had a collection of folktales he had put together which were very popular. We were always fascinated by the stories in which an animal as slow as a tortoise could win a race against a rival as swift as a hare. There was also one explaining why the mosquito always hovered around our ears and irritate us so much. Ms. Ear, the story went, who was quite a village belle, had apparently spurned the advances of the skinny Mosquito, laughing at him that she could not marry a husband who looked like a twig. She even wondered to the hearing of the whole village if Mosquito would even last a day longer. Since then Mosquito has been visiting Ms. Ear regularly to renew his marriage proposal and remind her that he was still very much alive.

"You did well in your test, Mr. Jumbam," the elderly one said, bringing me back to the room. Did I really hear him call me, 'Mr. Jumbam'? They must have seen the look of astonishment in my face for they all smiled. I was wondering why such an elderly person, who could even be my father, and who seemed so learned, could call a child like me, 'Mister'?

That was certainly not what I had expected in the interview room. The evening before, my brother's friend, who had coached me on interview techniques, had warned that some interviewers could be very stern, sometimes just to scare candidates and see how they could handle pressure. He had said I could fall into the hands of some mean ones, who could give me a hard time. Was I not lucky to have met people, who were not only friendly, but jovial as well?

A few more questions followed in which they asked about my class work, what subjects I did well in and which I found challenging. Had I ever been to Victoria? The answer being negative, they said the weather there was the polar opposite of what we had in Nkambe? I said I knew it was much hotter down there. Did I know where the wettest place in West Africa was? I said it was in Debunscha. And where was that? I said it was near Victoria. Then a few more questions came which I had no problem answering as they all hovered around Cameroon. For a while, they all sat in silence, each writing in his notebook. Then they looked at each other, nodded their heads and told me the interview was over. They asked me to listen to the radio for the results. I said goodbye and left as another candidate was being called in.

CHAPTER 4

PERILOUS JOURNEY DOWN SOUTH - 1965

Sacred Heart College, where the interview took place, was one of the best Catholic secondary schools in the then West Cameroon. It was under the strict administration of the Marist Brothers of the Schools, an international community of Catholic Religious Institute of Brothers founded in 1817 by Saint Marcellin Champagnat, a French priest. Their charism is to educate young people, especially the most neglected or marginalised. Even though it was not as old as the other legendary Catholic colleges, Saint Joseph's College Sasse, created in the late 30s, or the only girls' Holy Rosary College in Okoyong, Mamfe, created in the late 50s, Sacred Heart College quickly gained fame for its strong performances at the then London-administered General Certificate of Education Ordinary Level, establishing a record of academic excellence that has found few rivals to this day.

Its physical structures were huge and it was there that for the first time I went into buildings with several floors. The flowers around the school were immaculate in their diverse colours and the surrounding lawns were perfectly manicured. The fact that we were at the beginning of the rainy season meant that the rains had already purged the air of the dry season dust and given the buildings a thorough bath. They looked beautifully draped in yellowish and greyish colours. The rains had also given full nourishment to the earth and the flowers and green plants had responded in full force, blooming and blossoming and swaying from side to side in the refreshing breeze all around us.

Within a week of the interview, we heard the announcement of the final results on Radio Buea. I was on holiday in Nkar and a few days later, my elder brother, Joseph, and I travelled to Bamenda where we spent a few days, buying books and some clothes, bedsheets and other bedding which I carefully arranged in my brand-new box, another source of pride for me. We had been told that our uniform and daily wear would be supplied by the school.

A few days later, we boarded a bus from Mankon town for what was to be the longest journey I had ever made. We had been warned that it was not certain that we would arrive in Kumba, our first port of call, that same day, as there were numerous police and army checkpoints along the way. The government was then engaged in a long-drawn-out struggle to control the entire country from the rebels of the "Union des Populations du Cameroun" (UPC) party, and the western part through which we were to pass was the epicentre of the said rebellion.

As we boarded the bus, I could discern unspoken but contagious worries on the faces of travellers and their family members, who had come to bid them a safe trip. Our bus slowly rolled out of the motor park into the slow morning traffic. Soon it was clawing its way up the steep hill leading to the German-fortified administrative station where we met our first checkpoint. Angry-looking soldiers, toting automatic weapons, ordered us out of the bus, and we filed out and walked towards two other soldiers sitting on a small plank bench under an improvised shed of four sticks driven into the earth over which was placed two or three corrugated iron sheets. It was to them that we each presented our identification papers: a national identity card and a pass-card, called the "laisser passer". It was a typical French invention synonymous with the passbook black South Africans were forced to carry in apartheid South Africa. My brother and I had obtained ours from the district office in Jakiri a few weeks earlier. I was not yet old enough then to carry a national identity card, nor did I have a college identity card like my brother, who was in Form Three in Saint Joseph's

College in Sasse, Buea.

The soldiers would peer intently at the picture on the identification papers and then look keenly on the owner's face and back to the picture before handing them back without a word. They peered into my picture on the "laisser-passer" and then waved me on. When all the passengers had been so screened, they asked us to go. We boarded the bus and left. I could hear an audible sigh of relief from just about every seat. Some fellows then decided to further dampen the already low feeling on the bus with heart-chilling stories of soldier brutality against civilians. They said there were still checkpoints waiting for us where soldiers were generally meaner than those who had just checked our documents.

We drove along smoothly and largely in silence till we arrived in Santa village, the crossing point from the English-speaking side to the French-speaking side of our country. We met cars and Land Rovers and bigger buses already queued up ahead of us and all passengers had to leave the bus and trudge through mud, to another small hut a distance away, their travel documents in hand just as we had gone through some minutes earlier. We reached the small hut where some policemen sat scrutinizing the faces of the passengers and comparing them with what was on their documents. All around the building and in the nearby farms, soldiers could be seen peeping out at passengers, with fingers on the trigger of their guns. It was scary to imagine what could happen if those guns started coughing and spewing bullets in our direction. I was told that such incidents were not uncommon.

Everywhere I looked, I seemed to see and hear a soldier or a policeman shouting and threatening and barking orders at people in French. I even saw one soldier ordering a passenger in French to do something the young man did not seem to understand. Trembling with fear, he told the soldier in Pidgin that he did not understand him. For an answer, the soldier gave him a brutal slap to his jaw. The poor fellow bent down and spat blood from his mouth. That was scary and I was told that such acts of brutality were a frequent occurrence on the French side of the country.

We had all heard stories of people's heads being chopped off and planted on sticks along the road as a warning to those challenging the authority of the central government in far-off Yaounde that the government would not tolerate any dissent from any quarter. Several hours later, after stops and similar checkpoints along the way, some more stringent than others, we finally reached the town of Nkongsamba which was said not to be too far from Kumba, our final destination for the day. However, because of the delays caused by stops at checkpoints, we arrived around 6 p.m. and the fear was that we might be blocked at the last checkpoint out of the city as a curfew was in force from 6 p.m. to 6 a.m. When we reached the last checkpoint, there were tires and logs of wood serving as a barricade across the road. Two other cars were ahead of us. Our driver turned off the engine and stepped out, taking his car document with him. He stood behind the other drivers who were talking to the soldiers sitting on a plank bench at the corner. I saw one of them angrily shouting at a driver who had apparently offered too small a bribe. The driver then 'became more reasonable' and made an acceptable offer. The policeman, who received the money, openly counted it, turned and nodded his head to the soldier manning the barricade who flung it open to let the bus through. A similar scenario with the next driver. Angry exchanges and then the driver dipping his hand deeper into his pocket and offering a more acceptable sum. Our own driver, having witnessed what the others had gone through, decided to be more generous and was not delayed too long there. All the way to Kumba, he kept shaking his head and saying how difficult it truly was for anyone in public transportation in our country to feed a family. He had given away just about all his benefit for the day. What was he going to give the car owner at the end of the day and how much would he be left with for his family that was waiting for him in Kumba?

Even though I had been made to understand Kumba was no longer that far away, we spent what looked to me like three more hours, for the most part in pitch-darkness. It took several hours, that looked like an eternity, before we saw lights in the distance. Kumba was already within shouting distance and I could not wait to get out and stretch my legs. I was already totally exhausted.

The entire journey from Bamenda to Kumba had been dominated by long spells of silence that followed the tales of horrors of killings and extensive torching of villages and people's property in that part of the country. We could see it for ourselves. Villages were now only heaps of bricks and torn corrugated iron sheets. There was hardly anyone in sight. I wondered, as I listened to those stories, how anyone with a mother and father, a brother or a sister, a son or a daughter, could kill and mutilate another human being to the extent of cutting heads for display along the road. Did they not fear for their souls because killing was definitely a mortal sin? Did one of God's commandments not ask us not to kill anyone? But then what I saw at the different checkpoints where soldiers shouted obscenities at people, even punching some, as it happened at the second checkpoint earlier, showed me that those were people who could kill without blinking an eye. At my young age, and having grown up in a peaceful environment in Nkar and Nkambe, it was impossible for me to understand such acts of cruelty. I had never seen a corpse in my life, not to mention one that had been deliberately mutilated.

It was already well into the night when we knocked on our host's door. My brother was familiar with the place, having been there several times on his way to and from his own school. It took just a few minutes to greet our host and I was off to bed, waking up only the next morning when Joseph woke me up to take a bath and have breakfast. We spent a few days in Kumba during which time my brother met a few friends, some from his college and others from other schools. They showed us around town and we visited the big Kumba market that seemed to stretch for miles in whichever direction you looked.

CHAPTER 5

BUEA, HISTORIC CAPITAL OF SOUTHERN CAMEROONS

A few days later, we were on the road again, this time to Buea, the historic capital of Southern Cameroons, since renamed, West Cameroon. That was where my brother's school, Saint Joseph's College Sasse, was located. The ride was a smooth one. We went through large expanses of palm-oil and rubber plantations that stretched on as far as the eye could see. The conversation on the bus, unlike what we heard the day we travelled from Bamenda, was cordial and people could even be heard laughing and cracking jokes. What a sharp contrast from our journey through the French section, where the only conversation we heard was of violence and killings and maiming, with people's heads being chopped off and displayed on roadsides. Mercifully, we did not witness such a gory scene.

In Buea, Joseph was in familiar territory. He seemed to know every other student in town and one of his friends even introduced us to his parents, who graciously welcomed us into their home and allowed us to spend a week with them. We went down to Sasse where Joseph's college was located and he put his trunk in his dormitory. Then we went to BIROCOL, the Minor Seminary where I should have been had I opted for seminary studies. By chance, we ran into the priest, who had interviewed me in Nkambe, and I thought of him twisting his behind on the chair and farting in my presence.

Joseph reminded him that he had interviewed me in Nkambe and given me admission but that I was heading to Victoria instead. He said he was sad that I had not chosen his school but that he could understand why I would choose a tuition-free school over one that required fees. He then wished me success in my life. I thanked him and we moved on.

The weather in Buea was just as cold as back home in Nkar or Nkambe. Kumba had been stuffy and damp and smelly but Buea, with its foggy surroundings, bathed in a freshness that had something nostalgic. I was also lucky that a day after our arrival, the mountain, which had been sheathed in fog a good part of the week, suddenly unveiled itself, standing majestically erect and awe-inspiring. What a marvel to behold! I could recall the geography lessons Lawrence taught us in Nkambe about that mountain, how it was still an active volcano that could erupt at any time; how many times it had already erupted and how it was the highest peak in West Africa. Up until that moment, I had always wondered if there ever could be a hill that rivalled the Bambar hills overlooking the village of Ber where part of my family lived. But there I was, staring with gaping mouth at that massively imposing mount of earth that looked like a chain of hills and valleys that seemed to emerge from the flat waters of the sea, pushing their way higher and higher till their pointed head buried itself into the soft underbelly of the arching sky above.

Our Standard Six history books told us that thousands of years earlier, some adventurers from Carthage in Northern Africa had arrived at our shores just when that mountain was belching out smoke and flames, and they had named it "The Chariot of the Gods." Later, some Portuguese adventurers, in their incessant search for a passage to India, had made a stop-over at our shores where they found so many shrimps abounding in one of our rivers that they named it *Rio dos Cameroes*, the "River of Prawns." Succeeding European adventurers, misreading the Portuguese tales of their adventures, thought that name had been given to the whole land stretching from the Rio dos cameroes into infinity. Thus, the Germans, the first to plant their flag and lay claim to that region after the Berlin Conference of 1884, presided over by none other than their own Chancellor Von Bismarck, named the whole region Kamerun. When the turbulent Germans became a nuisance to European peace, the British and the French ganged up to throw them out from our land. The British then rewarded themselves with a small chunk which they quickly forgot in the armpit of their own neighbouring giant, Nigeria.

For their part, the French grabbed the bigger chunk, which they named "Le Cameroun français" and, unlike the British, who abandoned their own chunk in a neighbour's stinky armpit, the French pitched tent in theirs and went to work, carting away the produce from our rich soils and from our prawn-teeming waters for their own.

As foreigners rushed to grab chunks of our land, the mountain, which the natives call Fako, the abode of their legendary half-man, half-animal god *Efasa moto*, stood still and proudly erect, its tip tickling the navel of the sky above.

* * *

A few days later, we headed further south to the coastal town of Victoria, my final destination. We also ran into some of Joseph's friends who invited us for lunch by the sea where we could eat grilled fish. I was excited because I would be seeing the sea for the first time. I must have been inattentive as we went along because I suddenly found myself face-to-face with what looked like a huge flat glimmering sheet of something that seemed to be twisting and lifting itself from the ground as it rushed towards us. It was just a split second before that massive sheet, rising as if on its back, came crashing with an unbelievable roar against the rocks, sending fumes of water into the air. One of my brother's friends must have seen how astounded I was for he touched my arm and said, "Martin, that is the sea and it is high tide now; that is why you have those waves pounding on those rocks."

My vocabulary bank was beginning to thicken with new words: waves, high tides, low tides, canoes, ships, steamboats. As we sat waiting for the fish to grill, I kept watching the forward and backward movements of the sea waves as they rushed towards the shore with renewed fury. It was amazing to see tiny canoes of fishermen bobbing up and down those furious wave as they brought their catch to the shore. Some women were waiting, small baskets or trays in hand, to buy the fish.

The breeze the waves brought to us as we sat under a shade was refreshing. When the aroma of the fish hit my nostrils as it was placed before us, my taste buds seemed to jubilate as the first fleshy part of the fish touched my tongue. Joseph then warned me to be careful, for a small fish bone sliding down my throat could cause untold harm. They all concurred and recounted stories of people who had been known to die from fish bones that had stuck in their throats.

As I enjoyed the fish, I could hardly take my eyes off the dance of the waves on the sea. From our vantage point, I could see massive folds, one bigger than the other, rushing forward, with others pushing them from behind as if urging them to increase their speed, and then they grew bigger and bigger as they lifted themselves off the ground in one massive bundle before colliding with unbelievable fury against the rocks and disintegrating into tiny foamy pieces. Was that ever impressive! I did not then know that I was to spend the next four years in a structure that was perched on an escarpment overlooking that same expanse of water where the fury of those assailing waves was even more terrifying.

By the sea, I felt something I had not experienced for the few days I was in Victoria: fresh breeze. I opened my mouth as if to drink in the fresh air floating on top of that massive body of water. Elsewhere in the town, I was suffocating from the incessant heat, wondering if I was ever going to get used to it.

Joseph and I had gone knocking on the door of a family friend, Mr. Martin Kepe, whose wife was called Fanny. They were life-long friends of our brother, Kenjo, from the days he was a teacher of the Cameroon Development Corporation (CDC) primary school in Tiko. Mr. Martin Kepe worked as an electrician for the same company.

The CDC owned extensive acreages of banana, palm and rubber plantations and was the biggest employer after the government of West Cameroon.

The Kepe family and my brother were such great friends that when the Kepes were transferred from Tiko to Bota in Victoria, they entrusted custody of their first son, Peter, to my brother. The fact that they came from Ndian, deep in the forests of the southern part of West Cameroon, next door to Nigeria, and Kenjo from the savannah grass fields of the northwestern region, did not, in anyway impede their friendship, which I was to benefit from for years to come. In fact, the bond between our two families became such that the Kepes named their last child, a girl, Lucela Labe, after our mother.

That is the family that willingly opened their doors to me and I spent over a month with them before starting school. The Kepes were of the Protestant denomination and they were the first non-Catholic family I ever interacted with at close quarters. They were, however, very respectful of my Catholic faith and at no time did they interfere with my attending Mass on Sunday at the old historic Catholic Church in Bota by the sea. In fact, a few days before the first Sunday I spent with them, they asked a young man of my age, who lived with them, to show me where the Catholic church was, and he and I ended up spending a good part of the morning sitting on the rocks beside the church, picking up water-polished pebbles and tossing them out to the sea which was then unbelievably calm and meek. The wind barely disturbed the surface of the sea and all we could see were little ripples of the water that came to die by the shores as if too tired of their incessant rush for the coastline.

CHAPTER 6

MAN O'WAR BAY - 1965

The day our school re-opened, Mr. Kepe hired a taxi that dropped me on the spot by the post office where we had been asked to wait for the college bus that would take us to school. An hour or so later, the bus arrived with three other new students aboard. I was the only one waiting by the post office. I greeted those who were already inside; one answered joyfully, the other two said nothing, merely staring curiously at me. Shortly thereafter, I heard them speaking French which sounded strange to my ears. "Oh my God," I thought to myself as I listened to their conversation, which they carried out in low tones, "is this what I am getting myself into?" I then turned my attention to the student who had greeted me in English and asked where he was from. He said he was from Mamfe and that it was also his first year. The French-speaking students, who also turned out to be new, also seemed to be listening attentively to us speak English and I knew that they too were wondering if they would ever understand or speak English as we did.

The road wound its way up a small hill and then straightened up as it rushed into a frighteningly thick forest from which we only emerged several minutes later onto banana farms that seemed to extend as far as the eye could see. The driver, seeing from the rear-view mirror, how curiously we all looked at the farm, announced that we were passing through a CDC banana plantation. Then a distance away, there were long ranges of certain well planted trees that he said were part of the CDC rubber plantation. He seemed to enjoy giving us a guided tour as we went along.

The bus swung around a corner and there before us stood a huge structure that seemed to be perching on sticks. From afar, I could only see the massive upper section that seemed to be in plank. When we got nearer, it became evident that the lower section was built with concrete but the flight of stairs leading to the upper floor were at the front and I later saw that there were some at the back as well. Although the building looked freshly painted, it was clear that it was really old. We were to learn that it was built way back in the British days to house a naval academy that had its warships in the bay to which the British gave the name Man O'War Bay. At the front and sitting on another concrete slab was a huge canon with its voluminous mouth opening and staring at you as you approached the building. That was still a relic from the days when, we were later taught, Britannia ruled the waves as a formidable naval power.

Students dressed in khaki shirts and trousers loitered around aimlessly, scrutinising the new arrivals. I remember a student walking up to us and asking me something in French and when I told him I did not understand French, he then switched to English and asked my name and where I came from. When I answered, he turned to another group not far away and shouted: "Is Fon Rolly there? Let him come for his fox." What? Did he just call me a fox? What sort of a name was that? I wondered. I am no fox. I am a person, I thought but kept my thought to myself.

As I stood waiting for Fon Rolly, whom I had never met before, another young man detached himself from the small group and came up to me, a smile on his face. He was not much older than me. I was wondering who he was and how he could possibly recognise me in that place, when he stretched out his hand, which I shook. He said his name was Augustine Ndi and that he was from Tabenken.

"Oh, how awesome! You're from Tabenken?" I asked with excitement in my voice. He said he was aware that I had studied in his village and that I might be coming and that he was happy to meet me. He then took my bag and asked me to follow him to Fon Rolly's dormitory. I still did not know who Fon Rolly was but from the name I was able to guess that he was likely from Nsoland, and I was right. We met him, a much heftier and already slightly older guy, with a jovial smile and a slightly hoarse voice. He said he knew I was one of two boys coming from Nsoland that year. He then called another name, Zephaniah Yufenyuy Fai. Did I know him? When the answer was negative, he said he expected him in anytime too. He placed my bag under his bed and told me I would spend the night in his bed and that he would find out later in what dormitory my own bed was. I thought that was great and I was happy with the welcome. Augustine said we would have more time to chat later and I thanked him for being so kind to me.

I was still recovering from my first bout of malaria which had pinned me down on bed for a week at the Kepes. I had been told that anyone who came to the coast from upcountry was always welcomed by an attack of malaria from the omniscient mosquitoes that took an insane delight to feast on all newcomers into town. The one week I suffered from the malaria attack was hell on earth. I found the smell of food particularly nauseating and I gave mama Kepe quite some moments of anxiety when I threw up the moment the kind lady brought in food for me. She was beside herself with delight some days later when I started responding positively to the malaria drugs Mr. Kepe brought for me. I could now eat without sending everything back up again.

When I arrived in Man O'War Bay, I was still in the early stages of convalescence and I was only too happy to lie down on Fon Rolly's bed, waiting for him to find out where my own bed would be.

I must have fallen deep asleep before being awaken by a sudden slap to my face. I awoke with a scream, wondering if I had just had a nightmare due to the malaria attack. No, above me stood a young man, the one I had seen sitting on another bed a few feet away and who had watched us without a word. Our eyes met and he beckoned on me to stand up. I just stared back at him totally lost as to what was really happening. Words started flashing out of his mouth in rapid succession and all I could hear was "Debout, sixième! Anglosaxon! Debout!" He sounded mean-spirited and I just lay there wondering what harm I had done to him. I did not even know who he was. I had never meet him before, so why was he doing that to me? I still did not move and he suddenly sent another blow to my head which I blocked off with my fist. What was happening and why was I being so violently assaulted?

I had been told that francophones were always vying for a fight but why me, of all people, and in my frail state of health? Tears rushed down my eyes as my tormentor kept trying to give me knocks on the head which I kept blocking with my fists. I had not the slightest clue what he was talking about or what he wanted. I was getting desperate and yearning for help when another young man, who was about Fon Rolly's age, walked in. When my tormentor saw him, he dropped his fist and stood aside. As my saviour talked to him, my tormentor sauntered away, mercifully.

"I am Carlson and who are you?" he asked. I told him my name and said I did not know what I had done to that fellow who just assaulted me, unprovoked. I was in tears but Carlson assured me that he would make sure that it never happened again. He walked up to the fellow who had just attacked me and exchanged a few words with him and, before walking out, he turned to me and reassured me that no one would assault me again. I later learnt that Carlson was in Form Three, the highest class in the school. I doubted that he realised as he walked out how eternally grateful I was to him, and I remained a silent admirer of his throughout the four years we spent together in Man O'War Bay.

I went to class the next day where I met all my classmates, thirty-five of us in number. The French-speaking students were also thirty-five in number and there stood between us, what looked like an unscalable wall in communication. I was assigned a bed in the upper section of the huge building, the lower section serving as classrooms. My bed stood just between two French-speaking students and I thought it only had to be me to be sacrificed to people I could not even communicate with.

The first few weeks were not easy. At least my neighbours, even if it was clear that they too were meeting for the first time, were still able to understand each other but I could not understand a word of what they said, neither did they understand me. Then I discovered that one of them came from the port city of Douala and had picked up a smattering of Pidgin, which came in handy from time to time, although I had to make a particular effort to understand his own brand of Pidgin.

It was somehow comforting to know that I was not the only one struggling to understand my neighbours. Other English-speaking classmates faced similar communication blockages with their own French-speaking neighbours; and we knew they too were facing similar difficulties communicating with us. When we met in class or in the courtyard, we shared our frustration and wondered if we were ever going to understand French at all. It did not take long, however, for my self-confidence to emerge as I began to understand a little of what my neighbours were saying. Our class lessons also came in handy as all of us English speakers struggled through our lessons with the help of good teachers, especially an American, Mr. Woodbridge, who was married to a French lady, and they both taught us French. Augustine Ndi and other senior students told us Mr. Woodbridge was the best teacher to initiate us into the French language and culture, and they were not wrong.

One thing all first-year students were alarmed about was the ease with which some senior students, especially francophones, maltreated the new students. We all felt as if the school system had officially authorised the older students to brutalise the younger ones. When I came to understand that I was not the only one being targeted for maltreatment, I began to share my frustration with the rest of the students, especially my classmates. Even when we were told that first-year students faced even worse treatment in other secondary schools throughout the country, that did not come as any consolation to us.

We learnt that the situation in secondary schools east of the Mungo was worse than anywhere in West Cameroon. That such brutality could be meted with impunity on the younger students was unacceptable to us and we made it known to some of our teachers. The issue eventually came up for discussion at the level of the staff and an end was put to it. It was made clear that any senior student brutalising a younger student, would be dismissed. Although sanity did not come overnight, violence against new students did reduce considerably. The so-called "cutting-of-the-fox's-tail" ceremony, which we heard was compulsory at the end of each student's first year, did not take place with the English group, although the second year Francophone students did insist on it and actually inflicted some humiliating treatment on their first-year students, claiming that such a ceremony was an indispensable part of graduation into the upper classes.

***

I remember asking Augustine if there was a Catholic church nearby and he said the nearest Catholic church was in Victoria, four miles away. The school officials authorised the bus to drop students wishing to attend religious services in town, the only catch being that the students had to walk back to campus in the afternoon, making sure they were on campus before six in the evening, or risk punishment.

Augustine said we could go to Mass on Sunday, and I was delighted to follow him. My Catholic instinct took over and I wondered how students could stay away from church and not be worried they might lose their souls to the devil? For an answer, Augustine merely smiled and told me that we were not in a mission school and that I would soon get used to not going to church as often as I did in primary school.

The first time we walked back from town through that thick forest, I felt scared walking between huge trees that stood like sentinels along the road. Augustine and I had spent our childhood years on the open savannah plateaus and valleys of the northern grass field region, but there we were surrounded and hemmed in by trees, some as huge as houses and seemingly hundreds of years old. With time, however, I got used to walking back to campus each Sunday in the company of some classmates. I could not think of not attending Mass on Sunday because I had been taught, and came to fervently believe, that failing to attend Mass on Sunday was a mortal sin.

Mass was at the New Town Catholic parish church. Some Sundays we were dropped off from the bus just when the girls from Saker Baptist College, the only all-female college in town, were going to their own church in down beach Victoria. They walked in two long columns in their beautiful uniforms. That was how I always imagined secondary school children should look like, in clean and neatly ironed uniforms. I had never thought I would be saddled with khaki shirts and trousers as we had in our own school. I had seen how beautifully dressed my brothers and their friends always appeared in clean shorts and white shirts over which they wore sleeveless, jacket-like sweaters.

The Saker Baptist College girls looked resplendent in their immaculate uniforms with well-polished sandals on their feet. We would often stand watching as they filed past by and if, by curiosity any of them looked at us, some of us, the very shy ones, would turn our faces guiltily away. We, however, knew of some of our senior students who had struck relationships with those girls, some with already well-formed bosoms that brought to mind the catechist's daughter in my school days in Binju, Nkambe. The mere thought of being seen standing with a girl at a corner always scared the wits out of me. Although from time to time, I began to hear even some of my classmates talking about having girlfriends, we always doubted their stories. It was once rumoured that a classmate of mine was actually seen talking with one of those Saker girls, and we excitedly waited to hear what he was talking to her about, but it turned out that the girl in question was his cousin.

Before the year was out, we had become familiar with just about every student on campus, be they from the two upper classes or from our own class – anglophones as well as francophones. Our class was not called "Form One", as was the case in other schools, but rather "Sixième," following the French appellation. Everything on campus weighed heavily on the side of French. As our confidence bulged and familiarity with our surroundings firmed, the French language started to lose the frightening edge it had at the start, and we could hold reasonably long conversations in it.

In our fourth year, our two classes, anglophone and francophone, were merged into what was called *la Troisième bilingue*. At the end of the year, we all wrote the French *Probatoire* examination and some of us were declared successful. One thing that became obvious to many of us was that we all – anglophone and francophone -- faced similar challenges as we were growing up. Just when we arrived in Man O'War Bay, there were frequent frictions between the two groups, usually due to the arrogance some francophone students exhibited towards us. Not all of them, though, but a sizeable number did try to impose their will on us and fisticuffs between the two groups were not rare.

Some attributed the francophone behaviour to the violence inherited from years of war in their part of the country. Stories of killings, maiming, with people's heads being chopped off and displayed on pickets by roadsides were confirmed by the students themselves. One student, in particular, a loner, who kept very much to himself, and could often be heard murmuring to himself, was said to have witnessed French soldiers setting fire to a house in which his entire family was hiding. He was in the second year and did not come back to school at the end of that year and no one knew what had happened to him.

There was one fellow in particular from the capital city, Yaoundé, who seemed to believe that the mere fact that his umbilical cord was buried in the capital city endowed him with the luxury to bully those of us from our side of the country. He was finally humbled when the results of the *Probatoire* were released and his name was not on the list. He went on holidays and never came back to school, and we heard that he had actually been given the boot for poor academic performance. After him, humility seemed to take the better of many of our French-speaking friends, who seemed to realise that being born east of the Mungo, and receiving a French-oriented education, was no passport for automatic success in one's academic endeavours.

Our staff was composed mainly of French teachers, the principal himself being a Frenchman who was said to have been a member of the French army. He had seen action in Indochina when the Vietcong guerrillas humiliated the French army with a resounding defeat in Dieng Bien Phu. He was rarely seen on campus and his wife, a flirty-looking, heavily-perfumed, smallish French woman with heavy make-up on her face, seemed to walk on her toes. The principal's office and residence were quite a distance from the rest of the campus and it was only on rare occasions that we ever saw him. The French teachers were all members of what came to be known as "la Coopération française", the cooperation agreements Cameroon was said to have signed with France in various fields. There were only three French-speaking Cameroonians on staff for the four years we were in Man O'War Bay, one was the discipline master, the other the school bursar and the third was the sports master.

For the anglophone section, we had only three white faces, two British chaps who had come in through agreements with the British government as well. One of them, Mr. Brellot, taught us English, while his compatriot, Mr. Miller, a tall and lanky gentleman, taught us History, Geography and Civics. There was also an American peace corps volunteer, who taught mathematics, Mr. Barnow. He was around for just two years and when he left no other American voice was heard on campus again. A few years later, the English staff members, who were already of a certain age, left and were replaced by two other younger chaps, a young man, Mr. Black, who taught Mathematics and Physics, and a lady, Ms. McCrae, who taught English. All two were from Scotland. Ms. McCrae's presence in class always seemed to cause a sensation, especially as it was not often that she was seen wearing a brassier, which always gave her already well-formed breasts free rein as she moved up and down the classroom. Those bouncing breasts were a topic of much discussion and fascination among us. They tortured the dreams of many youngsters lost in that forest, with many of us leaving snail-like sticky trails on our bedsheets from wet dreams.

CHAPTER 7

FAMILY MEMBERS

In addition to the Kepe family, who had welcomed and hosted me in their home for over a month, I also had direct family members. There was my cousin, Michael Mbinkar, who worked in the branch office of the Ministry of Commerce, and another cousin, Kenneth Wongbi, a police driver. I would from time to time spend my holiday in one home or the other and I always felt very welcome. Michael was an avid reader of newspapers and magazines. There was always a pile of Cameroonian and Nigerian newspapers and magazines with colourful pictures and glossy covers, which I spent days reading. I would plow through them from cover to cover. I was always happy to follow Michael's animated discussions with his friends, who often came over to visit him, and he seemed to have a magnetic way of bringing people together. They could discuss politics all day long.

It was from their discussions that I came to hear of such African personalities as Dr. Kwame Nkrumah of Ghana, Jomo Kenyatta of Kenya, Milton Obote of Uganda, Julius Kambarage Nyerere of Tanganyika, among others. They found the squabbles among Nigerian political leaders particularly interesting and they would talk extensively of the actions of Chief Obafemi Awolowo, Nnamdi Azikiwe, Sir Tafawa Balewa and Ahmadu Bello of Northern Nigeria, among many others. He and his friends would often compare those Nigerian leaders with ours in West Cameroon, many of whom had cut their political tooth among their Nigerian counterparts in the days of Southern Cameroons: Dr. John Ngu Foncha, the then Prime Minister of West Cameroon; Augustine Ngom Jua, his assistant; Solomon Tandeng Muna, Dr. EML Endeley, the opposition leader, and many more. They would spend hours debating the merits or demerits of each politician and I listened to them with much delight.

Mr. Michael Mbinkar, my cousin. A politician to the core. Credit: Mbinkar family

A pile of another magazine, *West Africa Magazine*, printed in London, sat in one corner of the house and I read each copy from front-to-back. When he realised that I was a keen consumer of the papers, he brought more home and was always happy to discuss some of those political happenings with me when his friends were not around. Politics was in his flesh and it is therefore not surprising that he later joined the Social Democratic Front (SDF), Cameroon's main opposition party and was elected into parliament from the Jakiri constituency in northwestern Cameroon. Even when he was no longer in parliament, he remained an active member of his party until his demise on May 28, 2003.

Unlike Michael, my first cousin Kenneth took life as it came. There was nothing academic in him at all and he openly admitted that when it came to book learning, he would readily cede his seat to others. What he lacked in academic ambitions, he largely made up for it in his humane nature. He would go out of his way to help you in any way possible. Being a driver in the West Cameroon police force, his salary was not anything to write home about, but you would never have known it by how generous he was to others around him. He would come back to the barracks from the tiny villages lost in the creeks around Tiko with bunches of plantains, bananas, fish or fruits, which he liberally distributed to the families of the other three policemen around. As soon as his land-rover came to a stop at the door, the children would abandon whatever they were doing and come running up to him, dancing and clapping their hands and singing: *"Oncul ileh yayatooh! Oncul ileh yayatooh!"* To one, he would give a banana, to the other a mango, to another an orange. He would then ask them to go call their mothers, who would in turn come to receive a bunch of plantains, yams, or cocoyams.

I also recall a certain jovial woman everyone called Mama Mokube, the wife of another policeman, who was rarely around. She knocked on our door early one morning and said she had come to talk to me about Kenneth. "Dis your broda dey so, na some real man pikin. No bi dat mbutoko for my house. Soso climb for my ontop, he no fit even buy chop for house. Na fo hi akwara woman he house he di go spend money." When she saw how astonished I was, she said, "Na true ting ah di tok-ooh. Na some useless man, dat my man wey you di see-am so. But your broda na fine man pikin. Tellam say next week me a go bringam some fine, fine ngondere so," she said, giving a thumbs up to the girl in-waiting. I was surprised by her proposal and I told her I was sure my cousin would not be interested. "How man pikin fit be like he so where he no get woman where he fit cook fine chop foram?" When I told her I was the one doing the cooking, she looked at me from head to toe, and burst out laughing as she walked away. "Which kind chop you fit cook? Hear me badlok-ooh! Na fine ngondere fit cook fine-fine chop for he, nobi you," she said as she walked away still roaring with laughter.

When Kenneth came back home and I told him what she had said, he merely dismissed her as a crazy woman. But, true to her word, Mama Mokube did knock on our door a few days later, pulling behind her a visibly reluctant young, shy, barefooted girl, who looked like a ten-year old. As we gazed in astonishment, she said to Kenneth, "Na dis kind ngondere get for di warm dis house and your bed. Man pikin no get for bi he one. You bi fine man pikin. Take dis ngondere, na me a di give you. Na some ma siita hi pikin for village. You see fine bobi wey he don getam." She said squeezing the poor girl's chest that was as flat as mine. "You no see-am so?" she asked, this time directing the question to me. I merely shook my head in disbelief. The poor kid just kept her eyes glued to her toes, shifting uneasily from one foot to another, completely overwhelmed by the scrutiny she was subjected to.

Kenneth just laughed and told Mama Mokube he was not interested and that even if he wanted to marry a girl, it would not be one who looked more like his granddaughter than his wife. They left but Kenneth said he knew that he had not heard the end of the story. Mama Mokube would still bounce back, he said; and he was right. She came back, this time alone, but with the same pressing demand, urging Kenneth to accept her offer, even going as far as asking that Kenneth accept the girl for a few nights and decide for himself if he wanted to keep her or not. It took a while for her to finally throw in the towel.

Even with his low salary, Kenneth remained unbelievably open-handed and was always willing to send me money to pay my taxifare from school to his house. He would be waiting for me with a warm smile on his lips and before I knew it, he would be inviting me to jump into his land-rover for a trip to the villages located in the creeks around Tiko. I accompanied him several times to Misselele, Mondoni, Mudeka and other villages. We shared the meagre meals of the inhabitants, who were, for the most part, fishermen or labourers in the CDC rubber and banana plantations. Their openness to share the little they had with us was always truly heart-warming. They cherished the policemen who would come around from time to time just to make sure that all was well with them.

Some years later, Kenneth was transferred to Bertoua where he took ill and died. I still have many fond memories of the time I spent with him in Victoria and Tiko. Rest in peace, Kenneth!

* * *

Along academic lines, I was already holding my head high as I tore through those subjects I deeply cared for with relative ease, particularly the languages - English, French and Spanish. I also adored history, geography and biology. Mathematics, physics and chemistry posed quite a challenge to me. It was in Man O'War Bay that I began to nurse the desire to put my feelings on paper. I had read some of the things my brother, Kenjo, was publishing in little pamphlets and in local newspapers and I thought I too could do the same. During one holiday period in our house in Bamenda, I let my imagination fly away with me and I began writing poems in a twenty-leaf exercise book. That was my last year at Man O'War Bay and our school was being transferred to Buea and it was sad to think that we would not be going back there anymore. Even though we were being relocated to what at the time looked like ultra-modern structures, the Man O'War Bay of old was still clinging to me with unflinching tenacity. I found it hard to walk away from that isolated place lost in the thick forest that had been home to me for four years.

I decided I would not leave the old place behind without crushing my feelings on paper and that was the genesis of my first poem. In it, I recalled waking up one bright sunny morning and watching from afar as the humming sea raised huge waves that clashed against the unyielding rocks of the coast and how the resulting spume-filled waters rushed to die on the sandy beaches. Away from the violence and the turbulence of a sea in revolt, I also wrote of peace reigning in the placid gigantic trees around as they stretched out their enormous branches to the four corners of the universe. On the grassy carpeted floors below those ageless trees, I saw the soft rays of the sun, crimson in colour, bathing the glittering dew (the left-over of a rainy night) on the deep, green grass in a rainbow of colours. That sight-arresting scene had tickled the responsive feelers of my tender heart, giving birth to the first confusion of invading feelings that matured into my first poem; a poem in which I sang the beauty of the sun's rays fingering the sky-unveiled belly of a full sea groaning as if with child. In my first poem, I also recalled memories of how friends of mine and I would snatch floating coconuts from the deadly fangs of furious waves; how that rushing body of water would arch itself on its spine, like a cobra ready for a kill, before striking with determined fury the jutting, unyielding rocks of the coast. The bellicose waves would at times declare a precarious, unilateral truce. We would then sit on the spiky rocks to listen to the sharp calls of the sea gulls as they sailed in from the mirage-shifting horizon.

I recalled how we watched in the distance, the glittering, mystery-wrapped rooftops of Santa Isabel, the then capital of the Spanish island of Fernando Po, more commonly called *Panya*. It was from that island, historians tell us, that the first Christian missionaries, Baptist in conviction, had crossed over to our own land where they planted the first cross and opened the first pages of the Bible in our land. Others would eventually follow behind the same cross and the same Bible but with sometimes conflicting messages, all aimed at rescuing what was said to be our sinful souls from Satan's kingdom.

For our part, we often wondered what it would be like to live over there and speak Spanish, which some of us were already learning in class and enjoying its beautiful resonances. Before long, however, the ideal picture we drew in our young minds of that distant land was marred by news of how a few sons and daughters of that island had decided to visit mayhem on their own people in the name of political power. With that news, those once attractive rooftops suddenly seemed smeared with sun-caked blood, and the once so musical calls of the seagulls began to sound like the terrifying lament from the split throats of an oppressed people! Another corner of Beloved Mother Africa was being martyred by its own offspring! Many more were to follow.

It was not long before news of another human carnage began to emerge from neighbouring Nigeria. There, army generals were washing their folly and lust for power in the blood of the poor and the innocent. We often saw in the dancing horizon huge canoes, stuffed with smuggled goods, bobbing their way on the crests of waves as they set sail for Calabar in Nigeria. Why our 'ever-vigilant' customs officials failed to intercept them was a mystery to our then young and innocent minds. We always joked that those smugglers were perhaps not as visible in the vast shimmering sea as our tender eyes thought they were. Those were smugglers enriching themselves and their anonymous political protectors on a far-away human tragedy.

Even though we were still too young to understand the intricacies of the political football game being played in our backyard, our tender hearts were already beating in unison with those of the oppressed of the world. The raging sea, as if in protest over the senseless killings next door, would suddenly violate its own truce. My friends and I would then quickly skip off the rocks, giggling and mocking as the furious waves rushed for the rocks we were sitting on. When we were out of their reach, we would turn around to watch as those waves, in the felicitous words of a Caribbean poet, rushed to sink their teeth into the sandy beaches. Mother Muse, the legendary goddess of the poetic word, was already beginning to fondle the sensitive corners of my mind. I remember sharing that poem with my brother, Kenjo, who gave me a hi-five for it.

We returned to school for our fifth year to prepare for the General Certificate of Education, Ordinary Level (GCE O Level). During the holidays, our school was transferred from dear old Man O'War Bay in Victoria to a more permanent site in the West Cameroon historic capital of Buea. For the one year I spent at the new site in Buea, my attention was entirely focused on preparations for the GCE O Level that would crown my five-year endeavours at the secondary school level.

***

One classmate I was in school with, from Form One to university level, and whose memory is worth sharing, was Peter Agbor-Tabi. We were in the same class for the four years we spent in Victoria and for one year in Buea. We separated after the General Certificate of Education (GCE) Ordinary Level class, he, remaining in the same school in Buea while I left for the Cameroon College of Arts, Science, and Technology (CCAST) in Bambili. We had shared the same bench during our first year in Man O'War Bay and struck a friendship that lasted our entire life. I remember him inviting me to spend some days with his family during the holiday, which I turned down because my cousin, Kenneth Wongbi, the police driver living in Bota, had insisted I spend the holiday with him. One day, Kenneth asked me to accompany him as he was going up to Buea. I hopped in and told him I hoped I would meet my friend, who was on holiday at his brother's house in Buea. Peter always talked about his elder brother, Chief Agbor Tabi, who worked for the Post and Telecommunications Department and with whom he was spending his holiday. It was at his brother's house that Peter wanted us to spend our holiday together. Chief Agbor Tabi was an excellent football player and was a well-known man around town. Kenneth also knew and admired his football skills and was also eager to meet him in person. We did locate him at the Post Office and he gladly directed us to his house where we met Peter and his immediate elder brother David, a student in the Cameroon Protestant College in Bali. During our second term holidays, Kenneth being out of town, I gladly accepted Peter's invitation to go to his brother's house where I was warmly welcomed.

Peter and his family were from Mamfe Division in the southern part of our country that shared boundary with neighbouring Nigeria. People who saw us together often wondered how two people with such seemingly different personalities could become friends. Whereas I have always been on the shy side of life, often preferring flights to fights, Peter was the polar opposite: impulsive and irritatingly haughty and prone to swinging the fist at the slightest sign of provocation. Few francophone students who, for the most part, were so arrogantly imposing their ways on us for they felt superior to us, anglophones, could dare mess with him. He would strike first before asking questions later, if ever. He seemed to have an unbelievable ease with making enemies, and he regaled in it. But we somehow stuck together and actually had quite much to discuss together, often sharing class notes and preparing for tests together.

What few people knew, however, was how much Peter had been of assistance to me during the first two years of our studies in Man O'War Bay. I had frequent malaria bouts that were worsened by the quinine tablets to which I had an instant allergy. It would give me itches all over the body that left my face swollen and bumps on other parts of my body. There was a time I was seen more often in bed than in the classroom. It was Peter who would bring me food from the refectory and almost forced me to eat even when the mere smell of the food sent my stomach into convulsions, with even the little water I was able to drink bursting out of my mouth. One day when I had been in bed for three days with no signs of getting better, he rushed to the discipline master, a certain haughty French man of Corsican extraction, and told him they should wait for a corpse from upstairs, if the school did not act fast to take me to the hospital. Before I knew it, the school driver and some other students were lifting my frail frame from the bed and taking me down to the school bus. Peter himself asked to be allowed to accompany me to the hospital where I spent nearly a week, coming back as frail and as light as a cocoyam leaf. After that brush with death, I somehow felt protected by him. I sometimes wished I could swing a punch, verbal or physical, with as much ease as he did, but when the chips were down, I would back down and walk away, but not Peter. He and I stuck together, sometimes falling out in angry outbursts, then making peace and trudging on like all the adolescents of our age.

Peter was always at his best around people in authority – be it in school or in town. Being from a family of royal lineage, he and his brothers were well known and respected in the Mamfe community in Victoria, Tiko and Buea. Whenever we went to town, he would ask that we stop over at so-and-so's home, often a member of his extended family, who would turn out to be a highly placed official in the army, the police force, government, or in business. Wherever we went, we were always warmly received, and Peter would seem totally at ease with them, where I was feeling uneasy and wishing to get out at all costs.

He, like his elder brother Chief Agbor Tabi, the football star, had an easy way with girls which I found intriguing. They all seemed to flock around him and he changed them at will, a trait that never quite rubbed off on me. Around girls, I was shy to the point of paralysis where he would smile and converse fluidly and with unbelievable elegance. One day, Peter set me up with a girl from one of the secondary schools in Buea but I could not find a topic of conversation. We just sat in embarrassing silence, with me avoiding eye contact, until the girl stood up and left, to my great relief. Peter later told me that she complained I was too quiet for her liking.

In moments like those, I would always recall my first brush with love when the catechist's daughter in Binju, Nkambe, some years earlier, had taunted me with her smiles and her well-endowed chest which she had playfully pressed on my back as she stood behind me during choral recitals. Fear had, however, paralysed me from taking any action. Her memory would haunt me for a good part of my teenage years. I always wondered what had become of her.

When I enrolled in CCAST Bambili, Peter remained in the Federal Bilingual Grammar School in Buea where he wrote the General Certificate of Education (GCE) Advanced Level in the Lower Sixth Form as an external candidate. He succeeded and was granted admission in the Bilingual Degree programme of the Faculty of Arts and Social Sciences of the then lone Federal University of Yaounde.

When I also entered the same programme a year later, he was already in the second year which he spent in a French-language immersion programme in Dijon, France. He came back just as I too was preparing to go for a similar language immersion programme in Aix-En-Provence in southern France. Once he completed his degree programme two years later, he worked in a government ministry for a few years before proceeding to the United States, coming back some years later with a doctorate degree; I forget in what discipline.

He taught in the Institute of International Relations, commonly known by its French acronym, IRIC. He was to become its director some years later before being promoted to the post of Chancellor of the University of Yaounde. His reign was not an easy one as it coincided with government proposed university reforms that met with violent opposition from students. Peter, as the Chancellor, nipped those protests in the bud through what his detractors said was excessive brutality. But Peter was not one to apologise for his actions once he believed he was in the right.

His no-nonsense, unapologetic repression of that student revolt must have impressed and endeared him to the ruling prince who appointed him to head the Ministry of Higher Education in his government. Peter was to remain an active member of the inner sanctum of those who wielded political power in our country until his untimely demise on April 26, 2016. He left this world too soon. I salute his memory.

***

Then there was Mr. Conrad Ngalim, an economist who worked in the Prime Minister's Office in Buea. He was also a friend of the Agbor-Tabi family. In fact, it was when Peter and I were on holiday at his brother's house around Clerks' Quarters in Buea, that I met him for the first time. He had stopped by and when Peter introduced me as his friend and classmate, he shouted upon hearing my name, telling me we had family links from my mother's side, and that I was perhaps the only one from my family he had not had the chance to meet yet. He said he had just come back from Bamenda where he spent time with our elder brother Kenjo and wondered why he had not mentioned to him that I was attending school nearby? He then asked Peter to bring me to his house at the Clerks' Quarters before the holiday was over. From then on, I began to alternate, spending a few days at his house and other days at the Agbor-Tabi's. He and his young girl friend, a lovely lady of Bamum royalty, were always happy to have me over at their home.

Mr. Ngalim was an elegant and always well-groomed gentleman, who made it a point never to speak a word of Pidgin, always expressing himself in impeccable standard English, with a British accent to match. A meticulously rigorous civil servant, he ruled his office with uncompromising strictness. He was intolerant of sloppy work, either at home or at his office, and did not hesitate to sanction any lapses at work. He quickly gained notoriety for his no-nonsense approach to work and dedication to duty.

He was to suffer persecution later when he was appointed a district officer of a region, a post many of his colleagues would have sold even their mothers for, but, to everyone's surprise, he turned it down. He never made a secret of his disdain for political kowtowing by civil servants who, he said, were licking the boots of politicians for a pittance. It is said that when news reached the then Prime Minister, the Honourable Solomon Tandeng Muna, that his economic adviser had turned down his appointment, the shocked honourable gentleman asked that he be brought to his presence immediately. He knew how many people were yearning for that post and were literally wiping his prime ministerial shoes to be appointed district officers. When Mr. Ngalim arrived in his boss' office, the latter asked why he had turned down a prime ministerial appointment. His answer was said to have stunned his boss when he reiterated that the position to which he was appointed was for people who liked to tell lies. He did not want to deceive people by singing the praises of the Prime Minister's government, nor those of the federal government in Yaounde, when he was not convinced that what he was saying was true. His unprecedented rejection of what many considered a lucrative appointment made news around town but earned him the distrust of those in the ruling circles, beginning with the Prime Minister himself. How could a mere clerk look at the Prime Minister in the eye and tell him his government was telling lies to the people? What an unacceptable lack of gratitude to the head of government! To teach him a lesson, he was placed under security surveillance, and later stripped of his post as the Prime Minister's economic adviser. His salary was interrupted for no valid reason, and he lingered in limbo for many years thereafter. At times, he did not even have the money to fuel his old car, which he eventually sold. The ensuing hardship notwithstanding, he maintained his stand that the post he was appointed to was for hand-clappers who were willing to sing the praises of the government at all times. Even though he was rehabilitated several years later, he was transferred to Yaounde where, like most civil servants of his generation from West Cameroon, he fell into a depression. He spoke little or no French at all and hated his new environment with a passion. He was dumped at one corner of a tiny office in the Ministry of the Economy, with a wooden chair and an old table, and quickly forgotten about. It was there that he ended his career in the civil service, a sullen, broken man. Not long after his retirement from active duty, he died. What a man, Mr. Conrad Ngalim was! What a formidable personality, unbending and unyielding in his convictions, preferring hardship to compromising his integrity. A man of great worth who was literally hounded to his grave by political intolerance. I salute your memory, Mr. Conrad Ngalim!

***

One other person I met, and from quite an unexpected quarter, was a young Catholic priest of the Diocese of Buea, Reverend Father Paul Mbiybe Verdzekov. I did not go out looking for him but it can, in a sense, be said that he came in search of me, and in an unusual way. A friend of mine, Emmanuel Konglim, from my village, who was a year behind me in school, brought us together.

I believe it was sometime in 1969, when Emmanuel came to tell me about a young Nso priest he had just met in Buea. His name was Reverend Paul Mbiybe Verdzekov. That name did not ring a bell and I merely shrugged my shoulders in total indifference. That was my last year in school before the General Certificate of Education, Ordinary Level, and all I had in mind was preparing for it the best way possible, and there was no room to fit in a priest. Unlike Emmanuel, an exuberant, out-going individual, who was always much at ease around people of a certain class in Church or in civil life, I am rather shy and happy when I can pass anywhere unnoticed. Emmanuel was always at the forefront of encounters and took a boyish delight in giving details of his meetings with people, be they in the ruling circles of the Church or in political and academic circles. "One thing you'd really like with this young priest," he said, pulling out a copy of a magazine from his bag, "is this: *Cameroon Panorama*. He's the Editor-in-Chief."

Emmanuel knew how excited I always was when it came to reading newspapers and magazines. In fact, one of my classmates in our days in Man O'War Bay, once openly accused me of succeeding in my examinations through the use of a magic ring he claimed I must have ordered from India. Those were days when suspicion ran rife in academic circles in West Cameroon that some students were in touch with Indian gurus, who sent them rings that could make them disappear, or see examination questions before the teachers even set them. My classmate's contention, which he expressed openly, much to my embarrassment, was that when everyone else was busy studying, I would, more often than not, be seen reading newspapers and magazines in the library. But why, he wondered, did I always do well in my tests and examinations, when all I did was read newspapers and magazines in the library all day long while others, him included, were buried in schoolwork? How else was that possible if I did not use an external object, which could only be one of the infamous magical rings from India, which no one ever seemed to have seen but which many, including my accuser, claimed existed? I remember being shocked by his reasoning, which seemed to echo well in certain ears. Had he known that all those good essays for which I received so much applause from my English teachers had their inspiration at that corner of the library, he might have joined me for us to exploit those resources together. I did not let his negativity influence me one bit and I kept rushing to that corner in the library to pore over articles in the *National Geographic, Time Magazine, Newsweek, West Africa Magazine*, among others. Those magazines were, for the most part, very old but they still told stories I found fascinating. From them, I borrowed words and expressions that came handy when I was writing essays. Emmanuel knew my weakness for the press, especially as I was also on the editorial team of a slim school publication that did not survive the school censorship for too long.

As soon as I laid my hand on the copy of the *Cameroon Panorama* that Emmanuel had given me, I immediately browsed through the editorial. I was struck by the editor's daringly robust and virulent attack on the elections that had just taken place in the Bokassa-created-and-ruled Central African Empire next door. Under the penname "Barah Mbiybe", Father Paul openly denounced what he called the "election buffoonery" in that unfortunate Central African country. That was the first time I saw the word "buffoonery" and I immediately rushed for my dictionary, nodding my head in admiration. There again, my vocabulary bank gained one more word which I looked forward to using in my next class essay.

Those were the days in Cameroon when Ahmadou Ahidjo ruled the land with a heavy-fisted, "blood-and-iron" conviction. Under no circumstance did he take kindly to any views that might have been construed as a slight criticism of his rule, or that of a fellow dictator, especially one in his backyard, like Bokassa in the Central African Republic, or Joseph Désiré Mobutu in the Congo. We all trembled for Father Paul as we read his open denunciation of African rulers who trampled afoot the basic rights of their people. It was easy to see the fist-punches he was sending also firmly landing on Ahidjo's own ribs. We feared the state censors, people seasoned on intolerance and press bashing, would not hesitate to reveal their fangs to the young priest, sooner rather than later.

Monsignor Paul Mbiybe Verdzekov in his days as the Archbishop of Bamenda. Credit: Bishop's House, Bamenda

When I expressed my admiration for the magazine, Emmanuel smiled and said he knew I would like him. He then announced that Father Paul was coming to say Mass on campus. I looked at him as if he had just lost his mind. Our school was a government school and I could not imagine the school authorities letting a Catholic priest say Mass on campus. I asked if he understood the implications of what he was saying.

"I've already talked with the Discipline Master ("Surveillant Général"), and he's already given his consent. He's a Catholic, you know!" That was the first time I heard that our discipline master, noted for his sarcastic remarks, and who did not miss an occasion to send a well-aimed kick into a student's behind, was a Catholic. "If he's a Catholic, why don't you advise him to go to a priest and confess his sins of wickedness? That fellow is Hitler in disguise," I said, recalling one instance when he gave me a humiliating knock on the head in front of Form 1 students. Imagine a Form 5 student being humiliated in front of 'foxes'! For an answer, Emmanuel merely smiled and said the man was not that bad at all, and that I was just exaggerating what might have happened.

Shortly after breakfast the following Sunday, Emmanuel took a taxi up to Small Soppo and before long, a white Renault 4 car drove into the yard. I was still wondering whether to attend the Mass or not. But then curiosity overcame my resistance and I walked to the classroom where a handful of people were already waiting. A hastily improvised altar, consisting of a teacher's table, had been covered with a white sheet and another table at the corner held the chalice and other Mass accessories. Two chairs were put in place, one for the officiating priest and the other for the altar server.

When I walked in, Emmanuel, who was wearing the altar boy's vestment, came to me and literally pulled me by the hand to meet the young priest. It was clear to me that he had already talked to him about me, for Father Paul immediately came to meet me and, as we shook hands, he said, "Oh, you're Kenjo's brother, aren't you?" I noticed a shy smile dancing at the corner of his lips. I said I was, and he immediately praised my brother's writing skills, adding that he hoped I too would write as well as he did. I do not remember what my response was, but I began to warm up to him. He did not seem that bad, after all.

That morning, we all sensed that Father Paul was someone who took Holy Mass seriously. His homily was well prepared and neatly typed out. To crown it all, he suddenly, and unexpectedly, switched from English to French and delivered the same homily in impeccable French. I saw looks of admiration being exchanged in the room and I knew what must have been going through our minds. There we were, staring with open mouths as a young priest switched back and forth between English and French with such remarkable fluidity! And to think that we always prided ourselves as being the only bilingual Cameroonians throughout the Republic! Father Paul's language ability served as quite a lesson in humility to some of us.

No sooner had the Mass ended than Father Paul's language ability began to make the round of the school. Those who heard him repeated what they had heard to those who were not there, spicing their stories with elements of exaggeration. The result of that publicity was clearly visible the following Sunday when the room was packed full long before the young priest arrived. Those who came late crowded around the windows and the door, and the rest followed the Mass in the courtyard. At the front of the class, sat the wicked discipline master himself and I hoped the Holy Spirit would rub off on him and make him a more humane individual. He had obviously picked up rumours of the young priest's performance of the previous Sunday and wanted to be present to see it for himself, and Father Paul did not disappoint him at all.

In fact, for the rest of the year, the discipline master never missed Mass and he was always quick to cite the young priest as an example of a perfectly bilingual individual. He would always tell a student, who was fumbling in French or English, to go up to the young priest in Small Soppo for lessons in either French or English. Emmanuel, who was closer to the young priest than the rest of us, fed us with more of Father Paul's linguistic exploits, telling everyone how easily he could also switch from Italian to Latin, or German, or Portuguese at a moment's notice! Father Paul's reputation soared to the sky among the teachers and students alike. Outstanding among his visible traits was his remarkable simplicity coupled with humility. He would smile shyly before making a remarkably profound point in simple straightforward English or French, depending on who he was talking with.

The following year, 1970, I gained admission into the Cameroon College of Arts, Science and Technology (CCAST), Bambili. I did not know what had become of Father Paul until one day I heard on the radio that he had been appointed the first indigenous bishop of the newly created Diocese of Bamenda. I remember sharing that news with some of the students, who had been with me the year before in Buea, and one of them graphically described his appointment as a log of wood falling before a man with a sharp axe!

On the day of his outdoor ordination in Bamenda, I was among the several thousands of lay faithful, clergy and curiosity-seekers, who thronged the location. Even though I was a little too far by the side to see what was going on, I felt the intensity of the occasion deeply. I remember the then Father Pius Awa, who would later become the bishop of the Diocese of Buea, who acted as the Master of Ceremony, telling the excited crowd: *"Na wuna bishop dis. From now, Bishop Julius Peeters he power for Bamenda don finish."* The shout of joy that rose from that assembled crowd must have been heard several dozens of miles away. I looked up and saw the newly ordained bishop on a chair, a mitre on his head and a crosier in his hand, looking really majestic.

The dust stirred up by this ordination had barely settled when the Cameroon government made a dramatic announcement that it had arrested Bishop Albert Ndongmo of the Diocese of Nkongsamba for treason, a term which became synonymous with a sure death sentence in the Ahidjo days. The then dreaded Jean Forchive, Ahidjo's infamous torture-master, a man who once boasted to the world that he would not hesitate to torture even his own mother, if she were to be found guilty of 'endangering state security', came on radio to rudely interrogate Bishop Ndongmo. The sentence of that trial shocked the world: Bishop Ndongmo was sentenced to death, a sentence that was later commuted to life imprisonment under pressure from the international community. He was later 'pardoned' in what the state media loudly touted as the Head of State's unprecedented magnanimity; the only condition for that 'magnanimous pardon' being that the poor prelate leave the country, which he did, heading for Quebec in Canada, where he ended his days on earth. Irony of fate, the man who tried, sentenced and exiled him from his homeland, the dreaded Ahmadou Ahidjo, became himself the object of a trial for treason. After handing power to his handpicked-French-endorsed successor, Paul Biya, he is said to have realised that the French doctors, who reportedly told him he would die if he did not hand power to his successor, had actually duped him. He made the fatal mistake of rushing back to reclaim his seat of power, only to be chased off into exile and sentenced to death in absentia. He died regretting it. Irony of ironies, it was the same distorted justice system he had put in place and used with devastating efficacy against his opponents, that was used against him. Whereas Bishop Ndongmo lies buried in his Cathedral in Nkongsamba, Ahidjo, his arch enemy, lies abandoned on foreign soil. How low the mighty do often fall!

Shortly after his ordination, the young Bishop Paul Verdzekov led a delegation of Cameroon's bishops to Ahidjo on behalf of Bishop Ndongmo. It is not clear what they told the dreaded Ahidjo, nor what the latter's reaction was, but it is of significant historical importance that it was a young man, a newly ordained a bishop, who stood with courage before an unforgiving dictator to speak on behalf of a falsely accused colleague. I was glad I had been present to witness Father Paul's elevation to the rank of bishop of the Holy Roman Catholic Church.

CHAPTER 8

HIGH SCHOOL – 1970S

I witnessed the ordination of Bishop Paul Verdzekov when I was already a student at the Cameroon College of Arts, Science and Technology (often abbreviated as CCAST), Bambili. It was a very elitist school in its form and composition, being then the only intellectual hub of its kind in West Cameroon where anyone worth the name had to have studied. Admission was opened to just a handful of students a year. So, it was understandable that when some of us dropped anchor in its intellectual harbour in mid-1970, we were full of excitement. At the end of a two-year stint, a chosen few would proudly emerge brandishing the much-coveted General Certificate of Education, Advanced Level (GCE 'A' Level).

I arrived in CCAST Bambili just when the old administrative order, characterised by what some in high circles saw as undesirable laxity, was yielding its seat to a new administration led by a young Turk named Omer Weyi Yembe. He was a tall, bespectacled, and elegantly dressed relatively young man, when compared to the outgoing, elderly gentleman called Sylvester N. Dioh, who had dreamt of an institution in Cameroon that would have the freewheeling spirit prevalent in most universities in Anglophone Africa. He was one of those early seasoned educational administrators in West Cameroon with a solid grounding in British educational administration as practiced in Britain and its colonies, notably Nigeria, where many of them were trained. He believed in an administration that allowed students the liberty to supervise their own actions. The majority of students then were already of a certain age, many of them having been Grade II and Grade I teachers from government or confessional schools.

It was therefore not rare to see students neatly dressed in suits, walking with silent dignity around campus, looking more like darkly suited bankers than students! Then there were the elegantly dressed, high-heel shod ladies who, long after they had walked past by you, left the sweet fragrance of rich perfume floating behind them. That sweet perfume smell would obstinately cling onto your nostrils, leaving you sniffing the air and wishing you could hang around them much longer! It was not also rare to see young lovers who, as evening sent its fingers down to take possession of the land, would be seen leisurely strolling around arm-in-arm under the whistling pine trees. Some would be seen clinging to each other as they stood glued onto trees like mating ants, whispering words of love in the air, and giggling as fingers explored the sensitive parts of the body! It was fun to watch. The act of strolling along with a girl, or standing with her under a tree, was called "going to Tahiti." I never succeeded to know the origin of that expression. One generation seemed to have inherited it from the previous one and no one cared to know who had coined it.

The stuffy, centralised administration in the Ministry of Education in Yaounde thought the Dioh administration had ceded too much power to students and was determined to snatch it back. Omer Weyi Yembe (OWY to the intimate) was thumbed as the right person to clean the administrative cobwebs from the house and drum strict discipline into both the staff and the students, and he did not make any secret of what was expected of him within the two-or-three-year agenda Yaounde had assigned to him. He was a man on a mission and he was determined to succeed – at all costs, and succeeded he did, and with what brutality!

***

The presence of girls was a big deal for some of us, who had spent several years in unisex schools, and were then only meeting the opposite sex in an academic environment, and at close quarters, for the first time. The only contact some of us had had with girls was during the long holidays. We would come back to school, rivalling one another with lengthy and audibly hollow boasts of great female conquests we had made in this or that town, knowing fully well that no one believed that baloney because none of it was true.

Then we suddenly found ourselves in CCAST Bambili, the pinnacle of knowledge and academic excellence in West Cameroon, where girls of varying ages, sizes and beauty tortured our budding dreams. The girls we had only heard of, and dreamt about, were in their numbers and it was only left for those armed with courage – which many of us lacked - to literally reach out and touch them. Instead of drawing phoney pictures of imaginary female conquests, as we did in Man O'War Bay and Buea, and often leaving snail-like trails on our bedsheets at night, we were suddenly thrust face-to-face with the reality of matching such imagination with the facts on the ground – and many of us were tested and found woefully wanting.

One evening I arrived in the refectory to find at one corner a table neatly dressed with a white table cloth on which stood expensive-looking china and cutlery glittering on it. Assorted drinks and a number of lit candles took the centre of the table. What was going on? What did this mean? Questions summersaulted in our minds and floated through the air, unasked and unanswered. Before I could even sit down, a procession of neatly dressed gentlemen, in two-and-three-piece-suits, made its way into the refectory. Were those bankers or students? I wondered. They walked with measured, dignified steps, in a well-choreographed procession. Occasionally, one of them would pull out a neatly ironed handkerchief from his breast pocket, use it to wipe imaginary sweat from his face before putting it back. You could have heard the legendary pin drop in that hall as all eyes were fixed on them.

A second-year student sitting near me and having observed the unasked questions in my eyes, which were bulging with surprise, leaned towards me and, in a whisper, told me that those were the members of the Top Executive Club. He scanned my reaction keenly and then added that the club in question was one of the student clubs on campus. "Don't tell me those are students!" I said, disbelief waltzing in my voice. For an answer, he merely nodded his head with a smile on his face. CCAST Bambili was beginning to unveil some of its wonders to me. I then asked how many other clubs there were and I believe he mentioned two or three others – the Pacific Club, the Social Club and the Cultural Club, or something along those lines. But, from every indication, the members of those other clubs went into hiding when the Top Exco boys were on the move.

I searched the faces of the members of that table, hoping to pick out a face or two on which to pin a name. Yes, I could identify two former students of my alma mater, the Federal Bilingual Grammar School. Almost immediately, their excessive display of opulence accompanied by what I saw as unbridled arrogance arising from that table began to give me a repulsive feeling. I had heard stories of CCAST Bambili but I had always associated them with the fact that many of its students were already men and women of a certain class and age. After all, had many of them not served in various capacities in the West Cameroon government as civil servants, or in religious institutions as teachers, before gaining admission into that institution? If people who had been working before coming to CCAST had displayed such wealth, I would not have been surprised. But there before me sat young men, for the most part, around my age but who seemed too sumptuously flamboyant in their ways for my liking. For well over a month after that event, we seemed to think of nothing else outside our classes to talk about. For some of us, especially the former students of the Federal Bilingual Grammar School, who were almost always dressed in worn-out khaki trousers and shirts, the idea that students could openly display such arrogant and shameless signs of wealth was totally unimaginable. No doubt that many of us concluded that such a group was not for us.

***

However, as one month drifted into another and academic concerns took the upper hand, we all came to accept the members of the Top Executive Club as part of the tapestry of eccentricities that made CCAST Bambili what it was. We found the other clubs, much more subdued and crowned with an imbued humility that attracted us. Many of the Top Exco members, and by no means all, and not them exclusively, also gained notoriety for parading the campus with elegantly dressed girls clinging onto their arms. For some of us, who were scared of even talking to girls we were in class with, the idea of being seen walking around with one in my arm was definitely out of the question. To me and many other kindred souls, girls were to be observed and admired from afar. What if you were to ask a girl for a date and she said 'yes' and then you did not know what else to talk to her about. Memories floated back to my mind of the catechist's daughter in Binju, Nkambe, who had openly flirted with me by pressing her well-formed chest on my back, sending startling sensations shooting down to the lower parts of my body. Even with such openly flirtatious attention from a girl; I had been unable to reciprocate and tell her how I felt about her, much as I had wanted to. Would I be much bolder here where the girls were already of a certain class, age and sophistication? Not sure. To be on the safe side, I elected to play the role of a sideline observer, animating conversations in the grapevine where 'kongossa' could be paraded, polished and coated with a semblance of truth.

But, incredible though this may sound, I did become a member of the Top Executive Club of CCAST Bambili less than a year after finding the said club so appallingly distasteful. It happened that one day, and to my greatest surprise, one of the members of that club, who had been a year ahead of me in the Federal Bilingual Grammar School in Man O'War Bay, came with a friend of his, another club member, to talk to me. It was prep time and I was in one of the classrooms.

They asked if I could step outside for a minute for they had something to tell me. I did and to my utter consternation, they said their club had observed me quite attentively over the year and that all members were unanimous that I was good material for membership. I was all the more stunned by their request because, even though I had spent four years in the dense forests of Man O'War Bay with the young man in question, we had never had anything to say to each other apart from the usual civilities of 'Hi, how are you? Good to see you', etc. There he was, with a friend, telling me I had been selected to join the Top Executive Club, of all clubs? "You must be kidding me!" I remember shouting back. "Is this your own idea of a sick joke?" For an answer, they calmly told me that they would like me to join them and that they would give me time to consider their proposal. Then they left, leaving me standing there stunned for a minute or two. As they were walking away, I asked who else they had invited and, to my surprise, one name popped up which I could never have associated with that group either. I asked what his response had been and they said it was positive. I then asked for time to consider their offer. I wanted to find out from the friend in question if it was true that he had accepted to join the club.

He later confirmed that he had indeed accepted their invitation and that he would feel much better if I came in as well so we could support each other as we were not really sure what the general reaction on campus would be to our presence in that club. I told him I would sleep over it and let him know in the morning. I must admit that his 'yes' to the group played a significant part in my own positive response.

The next morning, I told him I was in as well. "You at least have a suit to wear when events come up, I don't have any," I told him. But just then I recalled that I did have a suit which one of my brothers had given me but which I had never worn. I had never thought of myself as a suit-wearing type. It was in our house in Mankon town. My friend later accompanied me to collect it and, to my relief, it still looked fairly good although some touch of dry cleaning and ironing could have rendered it much better-looking.

When I later met my sponsor and told him I was willing to join the club, he was overwhelmed with joy. He told me the new club members had not yet been officially revealed to the public because they had been waiting to hear from me. One day, we were all asked to be in our suits in the evening and to assemble outside the dining hall just when it was full. A table similar to the one that had so infuriated and repelled me earlier in the year, had been set aside for us and we were coached on how to walk, how to carry ourselves with grace, dignity and elegance. Those were the attributes, we were told, that put Top Exco members towering tall and proud above everyone else, and which the girls found so irresistibly attractive. I still had to pinch myself to believe that I was being really inducted (for lack of a better word) into the Top Executive Club of CCAST Bambili – and I was not alone. Just about all my classmates, and those who had known me in one way or another, were shocked to see me among the new Exco Club members. I knew they were all wondering why, of all people, I had joined it. That feeling was so strong that for some months thereafter, I seriously considered dropping out of it, worried as I was about what people were saying behind my back, and I knew a lot was being said that was probably not very flattering.

But then, for one reason or another, I began to notice a change in my approach to it all. For the first time, I began to feel some confidence sipping into me and into all that I was doing. All the coaching and mentoring we received from the senior Top Excos were beginning to take effect and, as my self-confidence bulged and firmed, I began to walk with my head held high instead of crouching at the corners of the campus and fleeing when no one was watching, as it had been the case in the past. I began to wonder why, on God's good earth, I had been so concerned with what others thought of my decision. What did it matter whether anyone approved or disapproved of my membership of that overtly exclusive club? It was true that I still occasionally wondered what my friends, especially the few who had come with me from Buea, were thinking; but I did not have long to wait, for some of them began drifting away from my radar of their own volition. That was their own choice over which I had no control and

I was happy I was able to overcome the accompanying guilt feeling I had initially felt on losing their friendship.

Several decades later, and with the privilege of hindsight, I came to realise and appreciate how much my decision to join the Top Executive Club of CCAST Bambili had been of great benefit to me. Out in the beckoning wide world, as I frantically searched for that legendary 'Golden Fleece' in numerous foreign institutions of higher learning across continents, I saw how much that club, which had seemed a curse at the outset, had contributed to build my self-confidence in many ways. While still in CCAST, I began to enjoy the feeling – not so much of superiority over others as of self-confidence and self-reassurance in all that I did. I later developed self-esteem, which was to serve me well as I struggled to ward off 'the slings and buffets' of life, especially that indescribable and intense feeling of loneliness in foreign lands, even when you are surrounded by friends of all races. Even though I never ever overcame my extreme shyness, especially around the opposite sex -- which still largely persists to this day - I did credit my membership of the Top Executive Club in those early years of my life for boosting my feeling of worth in many ways. On the academic front, I stood firm and held my head high, towering head and shoulders above many of those who were quick to write me off as a lost case, including some members of my immediate family.

***

Just as I was beginning to enjoy my new status as a Top Exco member, I clashed with the Principal, Mr. Omer Weyi Yembe (OWY). It happened in a strange way. Whenever OWY strolled around campus, you saw, but more importantly, you felt the aura dripping from the weight of his authority, which he wielded sometimes with ruthless efficacy; and I was about to fall victim to one of the first sanctions he meted out to a student. For some reason, I decided that I would smoke my first cigarette in life. I hated cigarettes and had never taken even a puff on one. One day, however, I ran into one notorious smoker, a classmate of mine who, as always, had a cigarette dangling from his nicotine-stained lips. He was puffing smoke into the air from his chimney-like nostrils and, after watching him for a minute, I asked him for one. He expressed surprise that I wanted to try one. I said I was just going to pull the smoke into my mouth and give it back to him. I just wanted to know what the cigarette smoke felt like in my mouth. We were standing behind a tree and none of us saw OWY coming. No sooner had I stuck that distasteful product in my mouth than OWY suddenly emerged right in front of us. The cigarette dropped from between my lips as I desperately covered my mouth with my hands. OWY immediately ordered me to follow him to his office. No sooner had I stepped into the office than he began to scream at me at the top of his voice.

"It must be one of you, Top Executive fellows! I'm going to show you that you are no different from any other student on this campus! This nonsense must end! You are the ones causing trouble here and I will put a stop to it, and that begins today, here and now! I am suspending you for a week. I want you back here next Monday and just make sure you don't show up here with that bush on your head and that rough goatee on your chin; they're disgusting!"

Before I walked out, he suddenly asked, "What do you think your brother, Kenjo, would make of this? That's a good man, a good writer, who seems to have raised a stupid brother!" I did not even know that OWY knew me to the extent of linking me to my brother. He was standing a few feet from me, his eyes peering at me from behind his black-framed spectacles. Then, he ordered me out of his office. "Get the hell out of here, and quick!" he shouted, and I did not wait to be told twice.

The news of my suspension quickly made the rounds of the school and I suspect that OWY himself was behind the propagation of that news, especially the bit about the Top Executive members whom he claimed were all orbiting within his radar. He vowed he was going to discipline and humble student clubs, especially the Top Exco, a threat he largely executed a few years later.

Even though my relationship with OWY did hit rocky grounds that day, he and I did not start the year on a rough surface at all. Far from it! I remember him sending someone to ask me to come to his office just within the first a few days after the start of classes. I wondered what I might have done wrong so early on campus. How did he even know me? So it was with some trepidation that I gave a timid knock on his office door. His booming voice answered and asked me to come in. I stepped in but stood at a respectful distance from his desk before he invited me to take a seat. He then pulled out a folder containing the General Certificate of Education (GCE) 'O' Level results and asked what subjects I was doing. I said History, English Literature and French. He nodded his head as he peered through the list on the table. Then he looked up and asked why I had chosen the arts and not the sciences? "I see your overall results are very good, even the sciences, except Chemistry where you had a fail grade. The rest are good: a 'B' grade in Math, two 'A' Grades in Biology and Human Anatomy. I don't even see such good results from students who have registered in the science section. So, Martin, I don't think that it is too late to switch over. What do you think?"

That was not what I expected to hear and I told him I had given due thought to my choice of subjects and that if I switched, I would likely face problems in the end. He said he understood but that I should know that the possibility to switch to the sciences would still be open for a further three months in case I changed my mind. I thanked him for his suggestion and said I would think about it, although I had no intention of switching over to the sciences.

When I left OWY's presence, I sat reflecting on my performances during my fifth year in Buea. I had always struggled with the sciences, except biology in which I excelled. I remember my teacher, a British lady, praising me in one of her comments on my report card, calling me an excellent student except that I was too quiet in class. That comment boosted my morale and I picked up courage and began participating fully in her class, which she seemed to appreciate.

I came to either like or dislike a subject depending much on what the teacher sent home to my brothers, who were my guardians, as comments on my report card. I was a good student of geography, which I adored, until we studied map reading. I was struggling to understand how to plot points on a graph when our teacher, instead of helping, took my graph book which he brandished in front of the class, roaring with laughter and calling me a disgrace. How could I not understand something as simple as plotting points on a graph when everyone else had it so easy? The whole class joined him in a good laugh at my expense and, when the opportunity arose, I dropped geography from my hands like a hot potato.

Another subject I struggled with but still had to write in the GCE O Level, because it was already too late to drop it, was chemistry. The situation was made worse when our chemistry teacher, a Cameroonian chap, who had just returned from the United States with a bachelor's degree, tossed my exercise book on the floor, telling me, in his phony American accent, that I would never go far in chemistry. I picked up my book, headed out the door and never looked back. I was therefore not surprised that chemistry was the only subject, out of the nine I wrote, that I flunked, emerging from my struggles with an 'F' grade.

I also suffered with mathematics, which was a compulsory subject in the GCE O Level. I decided to do something to change my approach to that subject. I swallowed my ego and went to a classmate of mine, Samuel Nji, who crunched figures with amazing ease. I told him I wanted him to help me with mathematics and I would, in turn, help him with the arts subjects that he found so difficult. The win-win deal was struck and we were often seen together, solving mathematics problems and poring over past questions in English, English literature, French or history. That symbiotic experiment worked like a charm and I hit a 'B' grade in mathematics while he too earned reasonably good grades in the other subjects he was struggling with. That was why when OWY pointed to my good mathematics grade, I could only smile internally and said under my breath, "If only you knew what I went through to get that grade, you would pity me and not ask that I walk that way again!"

At the end of my last year at the Federal Bilingual Grammar School, I had picked up end-of-year awards in English, English Literature, French and History. Those were subjects I did not only adore, but in which I received accolades and words of encouragement from my teachers. There was therefore no reason for me not to stick with them at a higher level.

* * *

Even though I was no fan of OWY's bismarckian 'blood-and-iron' policies, I came to admire some of his ways and actions. One decision I admired was his invitation to some members of the working world to talk to us and give us hints as to what to expect in the labour market once we got out of school. I attended two of such discussions with two public servants of the West Cameroon government. One impressed me, the other I found totally disgusting.

He first invited a Divisional Officer (DO), who reportedly was the first of his kind anywhere in the Cameroonian administration to have earned a university degree, or so he claimed. The hall was packed full when OWY ushered in our guest and urged us to listen attentively for the man was endowed with a wealth of experience that could eventually be of much benefit to us. OWY was effusive in his praise of the gentleman. But, to our greatest astonishment, no sooner had he taken his seat than the man lashed out at CCAST students. He accused us of not being 'patriotic' enough. He said the whole of Bamenda had seen that during the last march past ceremony in Mankon during a national event, we had marched sluggishly, with the boys showing off their beautiful suits and the girls exhibiting their expensive dresses. The fact that we were in CCAST, he continued, did not exempt us from obeying the laws of the Republic. We were showing a bad example to the younger ones.

We were all stunned for that was not what we were expecting to hear. Even OWY himself looked visibly uneasy, and I could see contempt on the faces of just about every student. The most irritating part came when students were given the floor to ask questions. The gentleman made fun of just about every question that was asked, claiming that we were asking questions more in Pidgin, than in standard English. He would then rephrase the question in what he claimed was good English before giving an answer. At one moment, he sat facing one of the windows, refusing to look at us in the hall. Some of us could take it no more and, as we streamed out, he suddenly sat up in surprise, turned to OWY and loudly complained that his students had dared to walk out on a government official of high standing. Did we not know that he could have all of us arrested and thrown in jail? Many of us did not wait to hear the rest of his ramblings.

A few months later, we were again told that another speaker was on his way to talk to us. With the thought of the arrogant Divisional Officer still fresh in our minds, it was no surprise that some students boycotted the new speaker. But I was glad I went.

Unlike the earlier speaker, there came a real gentleman, dressed in a dark suit, who stood up and bowed to us when OWY introduced him as Chief Justice SML Endeley of the High Court of West Cameroon. He acknowledged OWY's introduction with a gentle smile and then stood up and remained standing as he addressed us. What a sharp contrast with our Divisional Officer! You could have heard the legendary pin drop in that hall as the Chief Justice explained the intricacies of the law to us. We all seemed glued to every word that dropped from his lips. When his presentation was over, he received a well-nourished round of applause and a standing ovation. Then came the question-and-answer session. When a student asked a question, our guest would stand up to answer, only sitting down when he was satisfied his answer had been understood. At no time did he make fun of students' questions, even those that appeared to some of us as bordering on the ridiculous.

Weeks later, everyone still talked fondly of him, comparing him to the Divisional Officer to whom we all gave a fail grade. I left that hall wondering if I should not give serious thought to the study of law. Was that new thought going to mature and lead me down the path to a legal profession? It was still too early then to say.

＊＊

Another person who had a great impact on me was my English Literature teacher, Ms. Pamela Martin. It was through her that I first shook hands with one of Africa's, nay the world's, greatest writers, Nigeria's Chinua Achebe. Together, Ms. Martin and us, her young students, had pondered the tragic fate of the priest of Ulu, Ezeulu, that imposing personality, eaten by the hubris of pride, in *Arrow of God*.

Contacts then between teachers and students in CCAST Bambili were few and far between. I do not believe that Ms. Martin even knew who I was since I was just one of the over forty students she had in her literature class. But that was to change in an unexpected way. It came to pass that we had to go to town during one of the national day celebrations to parade in front of government functionaries and pledge allegiance to the flag. I do not recall which event it was but it all went well until things turned sour on our return to campus in the evening. The sand truck, commonly called a 'tipper', that the school had hired to bring us back to campus decided to dump us just after the bridge below the Catholic Mission cemetery in Bayelle. It had to happen below a cemetery, of all places.

The driver must have been drunk because he rushed with full speed down the hill leading onto the bridge, which he luckily missed. Had he hit that bridge, he would have dumped us all into the valley below and the story would have been told differently. In fact, as he rushed down the hill many of us began to scream and so did many onlookers by the roadside. The truck careened crazily down the hill, narrowly missed the small bridge before crashing against the hill below the cemetery. It then flung us with great violence into the bush nearby. It was a good thing that the front tires seemed to have stuck onto the muddy side of the hill they had struck else the truck could have fallen back on us as we lay on the grass. How we all survived was a miracle that animated discussions on and off campus for a good part of that year.

Ms. Pamela Martin, my high school teacher at the Cameroon College of Arts, Science and Technology (CCAST), Bambili, 1970-1972. A woman with a heart of flesh. Credit: Pamela Martin

I stood up from there without a scratch but without my glasses. I remember turning around, totally confused, searching frantically for my glasses in the tall grass around me. Then I looked up and saw as if the whole city was rushing towards us. From every corner, I could hear screams and shouts and before long hands were holding onto me and someone was asking if I was all right and urging me to sit down on the grass nearby, or to lie down still. There was confusion everywhere but my mind was on my glasses. Lord, what would I do without them? I hoped and prayed that someone would find them because without them, I was practically sightless.

Even though my glasses were found and brought to me the next day at the General Hospital, where some of us had been taken for closer medical observation, they had shattered under the impact of the fall. I was terror-stricken. What was I to do without my glasses? For a week after our release from the hospital, I walked about slowly and cautiously, leading many to believe that I might have sustained some form of physical injury. But all I was doing was measure my steps carefully so as not to run into anyone, or into a standing object around me.

It was at this stage that Ms. Pamela Martin came into the story. I do not remember why, of all the people around, I thought of going to her. I wonder if she had ever noticed me before – most probably not. She did not even know my name. After weighing all the options I had, which were not many, I decided that I had nothing to lose by going to her. She was the youngest of our teachers and there was something about her that made me believe she was the right person to approach, and I was not wrong.

One cold morning, a few days later, my timid hand gave a knock on her door. A few minutes later, someone peeped out from behind the curtains and then I heard the door bolts being unfastened and the door flung open and she invited me in. If she was surprised to see me at her door early that morning, she did not openly express it. I introduced myself shyly and told her that I was one of the victims of the truck crash and that I had lost my glasses in that accident. It was essential that I get a new pair, if not, I might go blind. I explained that I had brothers to whom I could turn for money but that they were all in far-away Yaounde, and it was not possible to contact any of them. I was sure, I told her, that they would send me money as soon as they were aware of my predicament. But, before then, I needed new glasses at all costs. If she could lend me some money I would surely pay her back as soon as I received money from my brothers.

I do not remember her asking me any question except to express her sympathy and relief that no student had been seriously injured or had perished in that accident. Then she asked me to come back early the next day, which I did. She ushered me in and gave me an envelope with a hundred thousand francs CFA in it. I do not remember what I said to her. Did I even thank her, or did I just seize the envelope from her hands and fled, eager as I was to go for new glasses? I believe I must have thanked her in my timid voice and then rushed off to

Bamenda before heading for distant Douala.

In Douala, I was lucky to remember a relative's home in the Bonaberi neighbourhood where I was warmly received. The next morning, one of the family members, a young man a few years older than me, accompanied me to an ophthalmologist, who examined my eyes and prescribed new glasses. The sigh of relief I felt as I fitted the new glasses over my nose was fathomless. Not only could I see well again but the new glasses shielded my eyes from the wind that had been directly assaulting them ever since my glasses were broken. It was only then that I realised how much I needed them, not only to see well, but also as protection against the direct sun rays, the wind, and the dust.

From Douala I was able to contact my brothers in Yaounde, who quickly sent me money by money order which I collected from the post office in Bamenda town as soon as I came back from Douala. It was with a grateful knock on Ms. Pamela's door that I handed her the money. I do not quite recall what I said to her as I gave her the money. I only hope my usual shyness did not prevent me from expressing my heartfelt gratitude to her. Why she had trusted me with so much money without the guarantee of ever having it back still baffles me to this day, nearly half a century later. I never ever forgot her for her kindness to me at that critical moment in my life.

**

One other teacher who left a good impression on us, the students, was our history teacher, a certain Mr. Aka. I forget his other names. The first day of class, we all sat waiting for our teacher, whom we were meeting for the first time. He walked in with his hands in his pockets, greeted us and looked around with a smile on his face. There was something friendly about him which immediately caught my attention. He then inquired if we had bought our books and that history at the Advanced Level required a lot of reading and that he was not so much impressed by passes in the class tests as by a good grade at the final examination set and corrected in London.

I do not recall what else he said but then, to my utter surprise, he suddenly turned to me and asked, as if he had known me all my life: "Is that not so, Sir Jumbam?" I literally skipped from my seat in surprise. When he saw the look of extreme surprise on my face, he continued to smile and then said, "Yes, I know you. Your brother Kenjo, who writes those literature books and novels, was a good friend of mine in our days in Kumba. That is where CCAST started, you know, and we were the pioneers." You could have knocked me over with a feather. That display of familiarity at a time when I did not even know the name of any of my classmates, that being our first meeting, endeared me to Mr. Aka for the two years I was his student.

His classes were very lively and his interpretation of historical events always seemed to carry a tinge of radicalism that was rare in academic circles in Cameroon of the early 70s where Ahidjo ruled the land with a 'blood and iron' Bismarckian hammer. The fear of being arrested and tortured to death as an opponent of the regime had such a paralysing effect on a whole people that few had the audacity to say openly what they felt, especially in the presence of people one did not know. It was rumoured that even among students, there were some who were not students at all, but rather undercover agents eagerly listening for the least dissenting opinion to have one arrested.

Mr. Aka seemed to have thrown all precaution to the winds as he interpreted historical events from a Marxist-Leninist perspective, which sounded dangerously subversive in many of our young ears. I once heard him declare loud and clear: "We are all the lumpen proletariat of this country!" Then he added that it would be criminal to remain indifferent to the brutalisation of ordinary folk anywhere in the world, be it on the frozen slopes of Siberia, with its numerous gulags in which the poor peasants were allowed to die of cold and hunger, or in the soot-infested factories of industrial Europe, or in the gas chambers of Nazi Germany, or even much closer to home, in the blood-stained savannah grassfield regions of Cameroon east of the Mungo, or deep in the thick, impenetrable forests of the maritime regions of Cameroon. We all trembled for him whenever he so openly castigated the brutality meted out to the poor and the oppressed right here at home. It was from him that many of us heard of the abject conditions of workers in what he called the dimly lit French and Greek-owned factories of Douala, the economic capital of our country.

He studied history at a university in Accra, Ghana, in the hectic heydays when the Osagyefo, Dr. Kwame Nkrumah, threw wide open the doors of his country to political exiles from just about every corner of Africa, including Cameroon. Being a member, or a former member, of the One Kamerun (OK) party, the traditional allies of the "Union des Populations du Cameroun" (UPC) in French Cameroon, he was said to be constantly under the radar of the security forces. The One Kamerun (OK) Party was created by the likes of Ndeh Ntumazah and the irrepressible Albert Mukong, who was then serving time in one of the notorious prisons in which the regime's political opponents were languishing, located in the arid lands of northern Cameroon. The OK Party had allied itself with the Marxist-Leninist inspired "Union des Populations du Cameroun" (UPC) of Ruben Um Nyobe, Felix Moumié and Ernest Ouandié. All those three resistance leaders had been eliminated by the Ahidjo regime with the complicity of his French masters. Ruben Um Nyobe fell under the bullets of the French army in the forests of the maritime region of Cameroon, while Felix Moumié was poisoned by a French secret agent in a restaurant in the Swiss city of Geneva. For his part, Ernest Ouandié was caught, tried and executed in a public square in his hometown of Bafoussam by the time we were receiving lessons from Mr. Aka.

He was the first person, to my knowledge, who successfully lobbied the London-based General Certificate of Education (GCE) Board to include African history, with special focus on Cameroon, in its lists of subjects at the GCE Advanced Level examination that year. My class was thus the first to write African history at the Advanced Level. It would not have been surprising if African history was dropped from the curriculum after our batch, especially if the contents of Mr. Aka's lessons became known to the officials at the Ministry of Education in Yaounde. His face literally glowed with pride whenever he spoke about Cameroon's struggles for statehood. Even though his active participation in the activities of the One Kamerun (OK) Party was a question of public record, he did not at any time mention them, nor did he gloat over what he and his comrades had been able to accomplish in the field before the axe of intolerance fell on them, sending many of them scampering for shelter in other countries. Many of us did well in history mainly thanks to his lively style of teaching and because the contents of his course were so relevant to the prevailing situation in our own land. I cherish Mr. Aka's memory.

My two-year stint in CCAST Bambili was crowned by good grades in French, English Literature and History at the GCE A Level, which threw wide open the road to the then lone Federal University of Cameroon in Yaounde. Another chapter of my life was closing behind me and another flinging its doors wide open before me.

My brother, Boniface and my sister, Monica around 1965. Credit: Family album.

The Jumbam family in the early 60s: From left to right seated: Joseph, Lawrence, Pa Mathias, Mama Lucela, Kenjo Jumbam (novelist), Monica and Boniface. Seated on the mat, from left to right: Denis, Sebastian (nephew), Tobias Wongbi (cousin) and yours truly. Credit: Family album.

My father, my mother, my nephew, Sebastian, my sister, Monica, and my brother, Kenjo Jumbam (novelist). Credit: Family album

My picture taken when I was in Form II at the Bilingual Grammar School in Man O'War Bay, Victoria, 1966. Credit: Family album

CHAPTER 9

FEDERAL UNIVERSITY OF CAMEROON — 1970S

My journey to the doorsteps of the Federal University of Cameroon began when I earned good grades in the three subjects I wrote at the General Certificate of Education (GCE), Advanced Level: English Literature, French and History. The year was 1972. Armed with that enviable certificate, I knocked and the door to the Bilingual Degree Programme at the Faculty of Arts and Social Sciences was opened to me. We were twelve of us in class, it being the smallest class in the entire university. The Francophone section of the same programme numbered around thirty-five students. We occasionally had some courses in common with them, mainly courses in French grammar, French literature and another in English; but, for the most part, we had many more courses with the students of the English Department.

Of the twelve of us in class, eight were former students of the Federal Bilingual Grammar School in Buea, my alma mater. When I left for CCAST Bambili after the GCE O Level, they continued their high school studies in Buea. We were meeting again after a two-year separation period. The first day we went to class, a French woman came in, introduced herself as our French language teacher and haughtily announced that none of us should ever expect to get a grade above 12.5 on 20 in her class. That was the first time we ever heard a teacher set a ceiling on the grades even before starting to teach; and she resolutely stuck to her word for the one year she taught us. We would soon learn that most, if not all, French teachers did just about the same thing. Mercifully, English-speaking teachers never set limits on the grades they gave us and that made life somewhat easier for us.

***

Among the teachers whose memory remains engraved in my mind, was the legendary Professor Bernard Nsokika Fonlon. What a man he truly was! A suave, polite, truly and complexly enigmatic personality, if ever there was any, totally seasoned in celibacy and in the humanities, having been thoroughly schooled in the rigours of life in a Catholic seminary in Nigeria in the 1950s. He had known and lived the exigencies that went with studies in other world-renowned universities – the Sorbonne in Paris, Oxford University in London and the University of Ireland. He was elegant in style, fluent in speech, a baritone that made all who heard him sit up and listen and pay attention. He lived a life of Spartan austerity even in the midst of plenty, especially when he served as a member of government. He was almost always seen in a worn-out *dashiki* for a shirt, with feet eternally clasped in flat-bottomed slippers. Anyone who heard him or saw him was almost always amazed by his dignified, slow gait and an ever shy and hard-to-discern smile on his lips. He was for a good number of years a member of the Cameroon government under President Ahmadou Ahidjo, a man who was more feared than revered, his human rights record leaving much to be desired.

Ahmadou Ahidjo was still very much in command of the country when I went to the university. It was often said that Professor Fonlon had stumbled by accident into the intrigue-infused political life of the Cameroons of his day, often baffling many a political colleague - the dreaded Ahidjo included – with his irritating insistence that priority be given at all times to the human side of life, which, as he incessantly preached, should always hold sway over the avarice of political life. While his political colleagues rode the latest Mercedes

Benzes, changing them as if they were changing their shirts, Fonlon obstinately stuck to an old German Volkswagen beetle which he drove himself until an accident, attributed to fatigue, forced him to reluctantly hire a driver.

Professor Bernard Nsokika Fonlon: A man of unimpeachable integrity

He was the head of the African Literature Department, which also incorporated the literatures of the black world (Americas, Caribbean, Europe, Asia). It was from him that we heard of the presence of black writers in the Arab world. He highlighted for praise, an Arab poet of African descent, Antarah ibn Shaddad, a pre-Islamic poet, famous for his poetry and adventurous life. His poems are said to form part of a collection of what is known as the "Seven Hanging Odes," poems of great beauty and solemnity that are said to be hanging inside the Kaaba, the building at the centre of the most important mosque in the holy city of Mecca in Saudi Arabia. He also introduced us to the poetry of the Russian poet, Alexander Pushkin, who was born into the Russian nobility, his mother being a black woman who had been taken to Russia to work in the home of a noble family and one of its members had fathered Pushkin with her. He also opened to us the world of great writers of African descent in the diaspora, particularly in the Americas and the Caribbean islands.

Among Professor Fonlon's traits of greatness was fair-mindedness in his dealings with students. Contrary to his French colleagues, he never set limits to the grades he gave his students. He always said that if a student proved to him that he or she had understood what he taught, he would have no reason to deprive such a student of the marks he or she deserved. We heard of French-speaking teachers who objected to his grading, claiming he was lowering the standards of the university by being so generous with his grades. His response was always that he was not rewarding mediocrity, but rather students who proved to him that they understood his lessons. For his fairmindedness and legendary humility, many students adored him.

He also gained international recognition when he founded a journal called *ABBIA Magazine* that gave ample room to researchers in all academic fields to publish their findings. He ran it for several years and readership was at its height in my student days. He ceaselessly worked for the creation of a class of intellectuals he called "The Talented Tenth," loudly echoing the views of one of his heroes, W.E.B Dubois, born an American in 1868, died a Ghanaian in 1963.

Among the other professors for whom I still have fond memories was Professor Paul Mbangwana. He was a soft-spoken, well-mannered and well-cultured gentleman, who taught us English and Sociolinguistics. He too was another fair-minded teacher who focused attention more on letting his students understand his lesson, and rewarding them for their efforts, than on the prevailing politics of student humiliation which many of his fellow teachers seemed to take an obscene delight in promoting in our faculty. I enjoyed his classes and that was one of the reasons I did well in them. There were, however, other lecturers and professors whose memories only bring pain and disgust to mind, and there is no need wasting valuable time mentioning them.

All said and done, the Faculty of Letters and Social Sciences of the Federal University of Cameroon in Yaounde was teeming with renowned professors of international repute. Not all of them taught me, though; nor were they all from my faculty. Professor Marcien Towa, for example, was a tall and elegant gentleman, who taught philosophy. He was said to have made deep inroads into the world of African philosophy, and was sought after the world over to give lectures in that field. I came to meet him at close range when he served as the assistant editor of Professor Fonlon's magazine, ABBIA. He gave public lectures on African philosophy which I always liked to attend, even though his reasoning was at times somewhat opaque to me.

Still in the Faculty of Arts, there was also Professor Thomas Melone, a French-speaking professor of African studies. Professor Fonlon took over the chairmanship of the African Literature Department from him. Even though Fonlon spoke highly of him, calling him his French counterpart, no two people could ever have been more different in their approach to academics and to life in general. Where Fonlon was a down-to-earth man, who had an open disdain for earthly glory, Professor Thomas Melone seemed to relish all that Fonlon held in open contempt. He was huge in size and tall in height, where Fonlon was of modest built and height. He wore heavy-looking-framed glasses with thick lenses and spoke French with a distinct Parisian accent although his voice sounded hoarse to the ear. He too ran a publication that looked like the French rival of Fonlon's ABBIA. He was the Chair of the African Literature Department from the inception of the university several decades earlier, and those who knew him well claimed that he did not leave his seat wilfully or with a smile on his face.

For his part, Fonlon always expressed admiration for his predecessor, praising him for conceiving the idea of endowing the university with a full-fledged department entirely dedicated to African studies even though only relatively few colleagues saw the wisdom in his action. The Afro-American, Caribbean and Latin American additions to his department's curriculum were entirely Fonlon's, and he revelled in telling stories of his encounters with black writers of renown in one part of the world or the other. Pride always exuded from his voice when he spoke about the First International Congress of Black Writers and Artists, which met in Paris from September 19-22, 1956 to denounce colonialism and its adverse effects on the black race. He was present and liked to recall some of those who attended, notably the heavyweights of Negritude: Aimé Césaire from the French island of Martinique, Leopold Sedar Senghor from Senegal, Léon Gontran Damas from French Guyana, Alioune Diop, publisher of the *Presence Africaine*, a well-known publishing house in Paris, among other Negritude adherents from Africa and the Caribbean. He also talked of the presence of English-speaking writers, notably Nigeria's maverick poet Christopher Okigbo, Davidson Abioseh Nicol from Sierra Leone, among others. From the Americas, he cited the novelist Richard Wright and regretted that his hero, WEB DuBois, was said to have been deprived of leaving the United States for political reasons. It was not rare for him to cite from memory sections from the works of the likes of Langston Hughes, WEB DuBois, Booker T. Washington, Countee Cullens, with relative ease, and would invite us, his students, to broaden our knowledge of the works of Africans, not only from the continent but also from the diaspora. What a noble man Fonlon truly was! A consummate intellectual and a rare corruption-free gem, floating freely in a sea of mediocrity and open graft both in politics and in academia in our country.

Another rather intriguing figure on campus was Father Engelbert Mveng, a Jesuit priest and a historian of renown. The first time I saw him, I was intrigued by his cassock that looked brownish and fairly well beaten. From where I came, priests always wore white or black cassocks, which were always sparkling clean. But not Father Engelbert Mveng, SJ, who commanded great respect in the world of African history the world over. It was hard to match the fame that the name carried with that man of medium height who seemed eternally dressed in a shabby-looking, brownish cassock that so badly needed washing and ironing. Several years later, he was to fall a victim to an assassin's bullet in his bedroom for reasons the justice system of our country has either failed to solve or has deliberately covered up – the former being the most likely. He joins the long list of murdered Catholic priests, including a bishop, that has largely gone unsolved in our country.

Across from the Faculty of Letters and Social Sciences was the Faculty of Law, where the likes of Professor Ntamack and Professor Stanislaus Melone, brother to Professor Thomas Melone, sat on the legal pedestal as their knowledge of law seemed to be on everyone's lips. The University Centre for Health Sciences, more commonly known by its French acronym CUSS, was located miles away from the main campus, in the neighbourhood of Melen. That was the citadel where the likes of Professors Victor Anomah Ngu, Jacob Ngu and Daniel Noni Lantum, among others, held the flame of medical studies alight across the continent.

CHAPTER 10

DEPARTURE FOR FRANCE - 1973

Those of us vying for a degree in Bilingual (English/French) studies were required to spend a year in a language immersion programme abroad. English-speaking students went to a French university in France and our French-speaking counterparts went to a university in the United Kingdom. Ten of the twelve of us in my class succeeded in our end-of-year examination and were therefore sent to France. Students in previous years either went to the cities of Besançon or to Dijon. Our group went to the southern university city of Aix-En-Provence near Marseilles.

We travelled together with our francophone colleagues by Cameroon Airlines from Yaounde and arrived in Paris in the evening. While they transited to London, we set foot on French soil. At hand to welcome us was an official from the Cameroon embassy, who took the bus ride with us to the hotel where we spent the night. It was good to see an official of our embassy welcoming students to France with such warmth.

We had barely settled down in our hotel rooms when we heard a continual grumble from below our windowsill which later turned out to be the fruitless protests from a drunk in urine-starched rags, clutching a half-finished bottle of wine in his armpit, relaxing in his own vomit and challenging to a duel an impatient tail-wagging dog just a few feet away. That was quite a surprise of a welcome in Paris of all places! Quite a culture shock as we had not then known that there too the have-nots slept in their vomit with tail-twisting dogs, salivating abundantly nearby, eagerly waited to clean up the mess. Dogs participating in the widely publicised Keep-Paris-Clean Campaign. The first of many such culture shocks that awaited us.

The next day we took the long and tedious but exciting train ride from Paris to Marseilles. The train cruised at breakneck speed, thrusting itself into the bellies of French cities, emerging from them just as rapidly as it had entered, and tearing through open and neatly manicured farms of the French countryside. It was a delight to watch the houses and farms and trees as they sped past by. However, trailing through our minds were questions we hardly asked but which seemed to be on everyone's mind: where exactly were we going? Who would be there to meet us? What would we find at arrival?

Several hours later, and just as we were waking up, a voice announced over the intercom system that we were about to arrive in Marseilles. Then, there we were in the old port city of Marseilles with its dense population, a mix of humanity from every part of the globe.

I came to know the city of Marseilles fairly well over the year we spent in the nearby small university city of Aix-en-Provence, thirty minutes away by bus or train. Aix-en-Province, or simply Aix, in the popular parlance, did turn out to be a pleasant city, bustling with life, especially among its ever-teeming student population from around the world.

Communism still found a favourable echo in the ears of many students throughout Europe, and France was a particularly fertile ground for it. There were those who swore by Lenin, others by Stalin while those from behind the 'Bamboo Curtain', Chairman Mao Ze Dong's children, churned out lengthy quotations from their Chairman's Red Book. From the Nippon peninsular, omniscient, camera-toting Japanese tourists could be spotted at every historic site. From continental Africa and Africa in the dispersion, African men could be spotted arm-in-arm with white women and inviting admiration with the wink of an eye. The starry-eyed white girls would recline in the hairy arms of their black lovers, defying the fury-propelled gazes of their scandalised society. Not to be outdone, white boys too with black girls in their arms necked in street corners or stood glued to each other in the shade of the tree-lined avenues of the city, looking from afar like mating ants.

Harvesting Grapes in Aix

Summer in Aix-en-Provence was full of pleasant memories for me. I enjoyed the splendid, sunny afternoons spent outdoors in cafés that were often overflowing with blue-jeaned, dope-snuffing students and tourists. I sometimes liked to talk with some of them, especially those with aimlessness peeping out of hazy eyes.

Those were the remnants of the "Hippy generation." They would often bum you for a franc and when you gave them one, they would give you a long lecture on how much the world would be a better place if we could all make love, not war. Many of them were drifters with torn, urine-oiled clothes who would sleep anywhere on the narrow sidewalks. Those were the casualties of the "Flower-Children Era", who could be seen sagging under the weight of drugs, alcohol and the stale stench of unwashed bodies. Unshaven and raggedly dressed remnants of the May 1968 University-Students-Revolution, staring with unseeing eyes into space, or loudly rebuilding, to the glee of the onlookers, the split hopes of those rock-and-insult hurling days in the fear-littered streets of Paris, Berlin, London, and other turbulent European cities. Not to be outdone, aborted poets and half-baked bards would be heard strumming away the eternity of poetic loneliness on out-of-key strings of graffiti-stained guitars, with stoned or indifferent crowd for audience. Then, there were the ever-present, summer-beautified, tanned and thinly clad girls invitingly pushing out their generous bosoms and spindle-like behinds in every street corner.

We did not spend the one year in Aix just studying and admiring the people. We all agreed that it was a good idea to look for jobs, make money and go back to Yaounde with the type of luxurious items we had seen previous groups bring from France and England. Who could come back from Europe and still wear the same old clothes and bottom-worn-out shoes as before? What if people came to visit you and all they saw were old sheets on your bed and worn-out shirts hanging from miserable-looking hangers at a corner? Where would be the difference with people who had never left Yaounde but who displayed much more attractive things to the public eye? That could not be. We all fanned out in search of jobs. Some friends ended up in a bean-canning factory. They talked glowingly about the work and how much it paid them. I stopped by that factory one day hoping I could also join them but when the smell of the beans hit my nostrils, I rushed behind the factory to throw up, and then left without another word. I became the butt of the jokes from my classmates who thought I was just a coward who could not stand the rigours of factory life, and they were probably right.

* * *

I then discovered farm work, harvesting grapes. That was more manageable although the vines, being at knee level, meant that one had to remain crouched on one's hind legs all day long. It was back-breaking work and I only survived there for about two months, then I was out job-hunting again, combing the city for what to do. Luck nearly smiled on me one morning when I went knocking on the door of what looked like a printing press. There was a man at a desk who beckoned me in and asked what I wanted. I told him I was looking for a job. He stood up, came up to me and surprised me with a firm handshake. Before I could recover from it, he was telling me how lucky he was that I had just come in on time to save him from an embarrassment. He took me outside where a small car was packed full of what looked like fliers and other products from his printing press located behind his office. I could hear the machines rumbling in the background. He said his delivery driver had failed to show up and that he desperately needed someone to deliver what he had in the car in different locations in the city. He showed me the key to the car and the map of the city of Aix-en-Provence and said as soon as I came back I would be his worker. He saw my hesitation and asked what the matter was. Did I not come looking for a job? I then told him I could not drive. He flung the pen he had in his hand against the wall, turned towards me in fury. I thought he would follow that gesture with a punch to my face.

"*Quoi? Tu ne peux pas conduire? Tu as quel âge toi?*" I told him I was twenty-two years old and that seemed to infuriate him all the more. He screamed that I had to be the greatest moron on earth to not drive at my age. What was I doing when I turned 18? You would have thought I was the cause of his driver's absence from work. Then he asked me to leave his premises immediately, and I did not wait to be told twice.

I walked away dripping in embarrassment. Up until that moment, I had never considered a driver's licence a necessity. There was a driving school not far from where I lived in the neighbourhood of Melen in Yaounde but I never thought of enrolling for driving lessons. That was too much of a luxury given the small stipend I received as a student. After that encounter, I walked up to a café a distance away to drown my humiliation in a glass of beer. When the waiter came for his pay, I asked if there was a driving school anywhere nearby. He said there was one just around the corner, on the next street not far from where we were. He said the owner was a good customer of their café during his break period and that he was really a nice man. He then asked if I wanted to learn to drive, and I said yes. He said he just had his own driver's licence and that the owner of the driving school would surely help me to get mine soon. He then warned me that the man in question was a retired officer of the French army who had seen action in Algeria. He was a no-nonsense man but a good teacher and that I would not be disappointed.

I left the café and walked directly into that driving school. As the waiter had said, the former army officer wore a stern look on his face but he received me with a smile. The fee for thirty hours of driving and ten hours of classes on the highway code sounded good. The deal was struck, I paid the first instalment and started the highway code classes that same evening. A week later, when he was satisfied that I already knew the rudiments of the highway code, he and I were out on the road.

He drove the car to a spot outside the city with few cars on the street and we switched seats. I was trembling as my hands held the steering wheel for the first time. He asked me to calm down and that all would be well. He said it happened to every new student and that before long I would be driving like a real pro. I needed that reassurance. Just as he had said, after a week of driving and taking highway code lessons, my confidence bulged and before long we left the suburbs to the streets inside the city itself. He seemed to like me because he said I was one of his few students who always showed up and on time for the theory as well as the driving lessons. With his encouragement, I was now the one taking out the car from its parking space behind the house, backing it up and bringing it to the front where he would hop in and say: "*Martin, allons-y, cher ami!*"

A week before the road test itself, I went for the highway code test. We had spent hours a week watching videos of other drivers on the road. We would identify their errors and learn from them. The highway code test went off without a hitch and I was given the date for the highway driving test itself. The morning of the test proved to be a disaster. The examining officer must have quarrelled with his wife the night before because he seemed to find fault with everything I did, and it was not surprising when he told me I would have to come back for a second try. Each student was allowed five driving tries on the road test. When I asked what would happen if a student still failed at the end of five tries, my instructor burst out laughing. He said in his long career as a driving instructor, none of his students had ever gone beyond the third try. They almost always had their licence at the second or third try. That was comforting.

On our way back, with me on the wheels, he praised the way I had driven and assured me that if I continued that way, I would surely succeed at the second try. He said he could think only of a few students who had ever succeeded at their first try. I paid for a few more driving hours and we went back to work. Two weeks later, I went back and this time there was a new instructor, a little more elderly than the first one, who seemed very complimentary of my driving skills.

When my driving permit came, I went back to the printing press where I had been offered a job before. The gentleman was putting flyers together in a box and when I walked in, he asked if he could help me. I told him I had been there about two months before and he had offered me a job but that I did not then have a driver's licence, and that I now had one. I told him he would never know how much his rebuke of me for not having one had motivated me to go for it. He congratulated me on my bold step but told me he did not have any opening then. But before I left, he asked me to hold on a second. He spoke with someone on the phone and then gave me an address of a friend of his. He asked me to go there and that they might need my services.

* * *

Thirty minutes later, I was standing in front of a textile shop in the old part of Aix-En-Provence, commonly known as 'le viel Aix'. I asked to see the woman he had asked me to meet and she turned out to be a really nice person. I later learnt that she had inherited the textile shop from her father, who had been a big textile dealer in southern France with an even bigger shop in the city of Nice along the Mediterranean coastline. She told me I would be making deliveries to customers in the city and that I would accompany another more seasoned driver from time to time to Nice to bring in more textiles for sale in her shop.

It was summer and classes were already over and I had all the time to work in her shop for some months before flying back to Cameroon. The most exciting part was plying the two-hour road to Nice twice a week. I enjoyed the scenery, especially when we cruised along the Mediterranean Sea, with all its beautiful beaches awash with families on vacation from the colder northern regions of the country and beyond. The company driver, whom everyone called Monsieur Jean, already a man of a certain age, had been with the company for well over twenty years. He was a pleasant, easy-going man, who was born in Algeria. His family had fled from Algiers during the Algerian war of independence from the French. To him, and to many former French inhabitants of Algeria, more commonly called "le pieds noirs," the only good Arab was a dead one. Each time he spoke against the Arabs and saw the embarrassed look on my face, he would then quickly say, "*Mais, je n'ai rien contre les noirs. Non, rien du tout. Mais les Arabes, je ne les aime pas du tout!*" If he expected me to applaud, he only got a stony silence. I did not sincerely know how to react in the face of such blatant acts of racism. Years later, I still felt guilty that I did not have the courage to stand up to him.

We would always stop at an ice-cream shop and watched half-clad women in bikinis come in to buy ice-cream for their screaming kids. Monsieur Jean, who had a reputation as a lady's man, would wink at me as the women walked in and out. Sometimes, as we drove back to Aix, he would boast of his sexual exploits in the city of Marseilles where he claimed he kept a string of mistresses. There were days when I went to Nice alone to bring back textiles to the shop at Aix. It was an enriching experience for me.

When the time came for me to go back to Cameroon, I actually weighed the option of remaining in Aix-En-Provence and enrolling at the university. The lady, who owned the textile store, assured me of a job that would enable me to pay for my studies. In fact, one of my classmates decided to follow a girl to Canada and we never heard from him again. After much reflection and soul-searching, I decided to go back to Cameroon and complete my studies at home – a decision I never ever regretted.

Back at the University of Yaounde, we resumed classes and at the end of a further three-year programme, we wrote our final degree examination. As we impatiently waited for the results to be announced, we loitered aimlessly around campus. That was a period of uneasy recess during which students made forays into neighbourhoods of low repute, with their bulging, rowdy bars where clients in varying stages of drunkenness mingled freely with women of light virtue, clad in see-through dresses, often mouthing obscenities and occasionally lifting their skirts to expose their wares to admiring audiences. As they squeezed their propped-up bosoms against you in those crowded bars, you would even feel the smart ones skilfully searching your pockets for some loose cash. That was why it was always prudent to hide your wallet in your socks for it could be snatched out of your back pocket within a twinkle of an eye.

The next day, we would then kill boredom by sitting around in groups and comparing notes about the conquests of the previous evening. We were, for the most part, in our early twenties and, being constantly in heat, the whorehouses were an irresistible attraction that served as a release valve for the pent-up stress of waiting for the results of the examinations.

Encounter with Dr. Daniel Lantum

One day, I ran into Professor Daniel Noni Lantum, a well-known public health specialist at the University Centre for Health Sciences, the medical school. After the habitual exchanges of civilities, he asked me how my studies were going. I told him I had just written my degree examination and that the results would be out any day soon. He then asked me to come to his office the next day. "Sure, I'll be there. What time?" Ten o'clock was the answer. "It's a deal; I'll be there," I said.

Ten o'clock the next day, my trembling hand gave a weak knock on his office door. Without even caring to look up, his secretary grunted: "*Qu'est-ce que tu veux?*" (What do you want?) I told her I had an appointment with the Professor. Could she tell him I was already around, please? I expected her to ask me to identify myself, but she kept her nose buried in her typewriter. Since she did not care to even look at me, I began to scrutinise her closely. Boy, did she have one hell of a generous bosom! She must have felt my eyes 'undressing' her for she suddenly looked up and asked aggressively: "Do you want to take my picture, or what?" I quickly said I was sorry. That Ewondo woman could be trouble; she could start a scene and there would be no end to it. Their reputation for picking quarrels at the drop of a hat follows them like the tail following a dog. But, I still could not get the picture of that well-nourished bosom off my mind. "You better watch it boy," I said to myself. "You could leave this office with a split skull from that lady's shoe!"

Shortly thereafter, Professor Lantum, who was in class, came in, greeted me and ushered me into his office. Walking past his secretary, I could not help taking another quick look at her well-endowed chest – what a generous gift from nature!

As soon as we sat down, he showed me a pile of documents, neatly arranged in folders, on a side table. "How soon do you think you can translate these for me? I've just finished a seminar/workshop on traditional medicine and I want the proceedings in English and French." Heavens above! Was he really asking me to translate that pile of documents into English? Even though I was in a bilingual degree programme and translation was my major, I had not expected to be so openly challenged to show how skilful I was in fondling our two official languages – English and French - just a few months shy of a bilingual degree! Had it been a document of a few pages, I could have told him I would try to get it done in a day or two. But there I was, in front of a pile of documents that must have weighed a ton, and being asked to give a deadline for translating them! Lord, have mercy! I frankly did not know what to say.

Professor Lantum saw my hesitation and embarrassment and decided to come to my rescue. "Listen," he said, placing a reassuring hand on my trembling shoulder, "take a look at them and get to work immediately. I will be here to help and guide you. I know you've never done this type of work before, but you've chosen this profession and I want you to excel in it. Come with me." He led the way to his secretariat, where his secretary was now loudly chatting with a friend, who had dropped in for a visit. "This is your desk. That is a bilingual dictionary over there; I know you'll need it. Get to work immediately and we'll see how far you can go before the end of the day. My secretary will give you some paper. Good luck!" And with that, he went back to his office. As I took a seat, I saw the two ladies whispering something to each other and eyeing me from head to toe. I decided to ignore them with a royal disdain.

* * *

As I browsed through those documents, it became clear to me that I was about to face my first baptism of fire in the field of translation. I was about to be introduced to the fascinating world of traditional medicine, which is what all those documents were about. Through Professor Lantum's persistent effort, the Ministry of Public Health had empowered him to carry out a census of traditional healers in Cameroon. As the weeks went by, many of them paraded in and out of the Professor's office from every corner of the Republic. The list of the diseases each of them claimed to treat ran into several dozens. A few of them were from my part of the country. One of them, in particular, was from my village and listed nearly forty diseases he claimed he could cure, the majority of them being sex-related: gonorrhoea, syphilis, "piss-tie-face," among others. Had HIV-AIDS been around in those days, I am sure he would have had it on his list as well.

He once told me a fascinating story, hard to verify, about someone who was then a minister in the government. He claimed the man had just placed him on a monthly salary. I asked what he had done for him to be so honoured. "Don't you know his wife had abandoned him?" That was news to me. And why would she do that to the poor man? I inquired. "You know women. That man's enemies had rendered his *weewee* a mere stunted growth between his legs, good only for passing out water. When he consulted me, I merely touched it with this stick," he showed me a short wooden stick entirely covered with a hairy animal skin, which he claimed was from the scrotum of a buffalo. "Yes, when this stick touched his *baabaa,* I saw wonders; it immediately sprang to attention and the man had to rush to some free girls in Briqueterie and it took the joint efforts of three of them to quell it down. From that day, I've become his worker. He pays me whenever I ask him for money. Don't you know that he now has a new wife, young and plumb? It's thanks to me!" he said, smiling proudly.

I heard all kinds of stories from those traditional healers, one as fascinating as the other. Be they men or women, they all claimed to perform miracles, especially in below-the-navel activities. I remember one of them in particular who came from Ebolowa, carrying a bag I assumed contained some medicinal herbs and trailing behind him a relatively young and nice-looking girl. As soon as they walked in, he looked around, sniffing the air with suspicion and peering at the corners of the office. When I asked what he was doing, he leaned over my desk and told me *"mon fils, c'est pour m'assurer qu'il n'y a pas de mauvais esprits ici"* (my son, I just want to make sure that there are no evil spirits here). When he saw the look of astonishment on my face, he burst out laughing. I could not help laughing myself.

I asked him what his specialty was. He looked around to make sure no one was looking and then made a gesture with his right hand to the lower part of his body, which carried the weight of obscenity. He then leaned towards me and asked to know the last time I had gone with a woman. Without even waiting for an answer, he beckoned his companion to give him his bag. Opening it, he took out a small bottle with a white powdery substance in it. "All you need to do is sprinkle this in the direction of the woman you want, and she'll follow you like a sheep," he said, with a knowing wink. I took the bottle from him, scrutinised it for a minute and then turned round to look at his companion. He looked up in surprise, rightly guessing what I had in mind, then quickly seized the bottle from my hand, screaming with laughter and shaking his head disapprovingly: "No, no, not with her! You're a dangerous man. If you buy it from me, you have to go to someone else, not her!" With that, he quickly stood up and led his companion out of the office, and I could hear him telling her how dangerous the young men in the capital city are. I never saw him again.

***

A few days into my translation work with Professor Lantum, my confidence started to swell and bubble over. What I had at first thought I could not do, I was now doing well, and loving it. In fact, I began to churn out several pages of hand-written translation that the professor's secretary could not or was not willing to handle. She started complaining of not being able to do the office work for which she was employed because of the translation. "And, by the way, was I employed to type work in English? Have I not always asked to be sent to study English but has anyone ever listened to me? Now I am being asked to type long English texts. It has to be me since I was born unlucky. In other offices, secretaries are being paid for doing nothing; when it comes to me, I have to toil and labour under a ton of work, and more is still being added to it; and this for what? For a pittance!"

I remember telling Professor Lantum that his secretary was not happy with the work and he did the right thing by employing the services of a temporary English-speaking secretary with whom I worked well. She came in two days a week, enough time for me to translate chunks of documents for typing. However, no sooner had she started work than the professor's secretary found another reason to grumble. Why was all the money for the project being given to others while those of them in the office had nothing? She was an eternal complainer. I just had to ignore her, if I was to do any work at all.

The most memorable part of the work I did for Professor Lantum was the pay I received at the end of the month. He called me into his office and handed me an envelope. When he saw how confused I was, he said: "That's your pay. You've done commendable work for me and I'm glad I hired you." I wondered if he saw how much my hands trembled as I held onto that envelope. I did not frankly know what to say or do. He and I had not even discussed how much he was to pay me and if he had given me any amount, no matter how small, I would still have been happy. But to give me up to 50.000 francs was simply unbelievable. That sum in 1976 would be worth 500.000 francs today!

I remember clutching that envelop in my trembling hands and heading for Melen where my brother, Kenjo, and his family lived. I showed him the money, told him Professor Lantum had just paid me for the work I had been doing for him. I told him I had not expected to be given such an amount for the work I had done for him. My brother shared my joy and said he had always known Doctor Dan to be a good man. He congratulated me on doing good work and being honourably rewarded for it.

I was successful in my degree examination and was awarded a Bachelor of Arts Degree in Bilingual Studies. In the late seventies, jobs were easy to come by, especially for Bilingual Degree holders. I remember dropping applications for a job at the National Assembly and at the Presidency of the Republic. Some friends of mine, who leaned towards teaching, took the road to the Higher Teacher Training College, known in French as "Ecole Normale Superieure", where they were given admission on the spot. Since I was also thinking of trying my hand in journalism, if the Presidency or the National Assembly did not give me room among their translators and interpreters, I went to ESIJY (the Yaounde School of Journalism) where Professor Chindje Kouleu was teaching. I had met him in Aix-en-Provence in southern France two years earlier. He had left shortly after our arrival to come back to Cameroon where he got a job in ESIJY. When we came back from France, I met him a few times and he thought I was good material for journalism.

CHAPTER 11

BACK TO EUROPE

I remember telling Professor Lantum that I was looking forward to working either at the Presidency of the Republic or at the National Assembly. It was easier for translators working in those two institutions to be sent abroad for further studies than those who were employed and sent to work in the various ministries where they were practically buried in a "garage" and no one ever thought of sending them for further studies. He said he wished he could keep me on a permanent basis in his department but that there was no budget for it. In the meantime, he said, I could still remain with him pending something more permanent. In early September 1976, I received word, through my friend and brother, John Sabbas Bime, 'John B', to the intimate, that I was wanted at the Linguistics Services of the Presidency of the Republic. John was already a seasoned translator and conference interpreter there.

On the appointed day and hour, I was standing in front of the main entrance into the Presidential Palace. After going through several layers of security screening by guards, who seemed as if a smile had never crossed their lips, I was ushered, trembling like a leaf, into the translation office of the Linguistics Services where a certain French lady, Mrs. Atangana and Mr. William Mbelem met me. They said they had received my curriculum vitae and seen that I once studied Spanish. I told them I had received a pass grade in Spanish at the London General Certificate of Education Ordinary Level at the Bilingual Grammar School in Man O'War Bay, but that my Spanish, for lack of use, had become fairly rusty. They said that did not matter and immediately gave me a piece of paper on which I was asked to write an application to the Secretary General of the Presidency of the Republic for a scholarship to study Spanish in Madrid. The plan was that from Madrid I would then proceed to either Paris, Washington DC or Canada for translation and interpretation studies. That was the most amazing thing in my life. It was surreal. There I was, inside the Presidency of the Republic, the citadel of supreme power in Cameroon under the dreaded Ahmadou Ahidjo, who, at that moment, was perhaps just a few feet away from me. I even thought I could feel his breath on my neck. Boy, was I ever eager to get out of there!

Confusion ran riot on my face and in my mind. Had it not been for the presence of my friend and brother, John Bime, I would have told them I was still going to think about it. As I sat in one room alone, in front of the virgin paper, wondering what to do, John walked in and congratulated me and laughed my confusion away. "Go for it!" he said. That was when I wrote the application. Before I left, I was told to prepare to leave for Madrid in a week's time. Just enough time for me to get my passport renewed and I would be leaving. I was sent with a note to the frontier police where I was asked if I had a passport. The answer being affirmative I was asked to go for it and bring it back before the close of business that same day. I took a taxi back to my room at the students' residential area and was back with it in a matter of hours. I was asked to come back the next day. I left from there wondering if I was not dreaming. Was that really happening in Cameroon, of all places? Passports were a rare commodity in those days and I had one simply because I had travelled to France two years earlier as part of the language immersion programme students of the Bilingual Studies programme undertook during their second year.

With confusion running amok in my mind, I went back to the office to tell Professor Lantum what had happened and how confused I was. He wondered why I was confused. He rose from his seat, came forward and gave me a big hug, saying how proud he was of me. He said he knew I was made for great things and that I should go back home, pack my things and be ready to go for it. His hearty congratulation greatly oiled the hinges of my self-confidence. But one thing still bothered me, though; no family member of mine was around, my brother, Kenjo, having been transferred to Bamenda some months earlier. I felt uncomfortably lonely but Professor Lantum's reassuring words came as a balm to my heart. He said he would let my brother know of the circumstances under which I had to leave the country. We were in Cameroon of the late 1970s and the phone was a luxury few could afford. Even though Professor Lantum had one in his office, my brother had been transferred to a school in Bamenda where the availability of phones was still a pipe dream.

***

The next day, I collected my passport from the immigration office and went back to the Presidency where I was given an air-ticket and instructed to go to the Spanish embassy with my passport for a visa. I took a taxi to the Spanish embassy where I deposited my passport and was asked to come for it early the next day. Early the next day, I collected the passport that bore the Spanish visa, an indication that I was given entry into Madrid. Was that a dream or reality?

A few days to my departure, Professor Fonlon sent for me. I met him in his office at Ngoa-Ekelle and he said he had heard I was about to leave for Spain. I said that was correct. He then informed me that he had been eyeing me for a teaching position in his department and that he thought it was not too late for me to cancel my departure for Madrid and accept his offer. He assured me he would do all in his power to get me a scholarship or a grant for studies that would lead to a doctorate degree from an American university.

Some months earlier, he and I had discussed the possibility of my applying for a position in an American university for Afro-American studies with the view to coming back and teaching in his department.

Earlier, we had even toyed with the idea of my applying for admission to a university in Cairo, Egypt, to study Arabic. His contention was that there was a lot written in Arabic by Cameroonian Moslem scholars in North Cameroon that still laid fallow and out of reach of academic analysis. It had always been his dream to have such material translated into English and French and put at the disposal of the academic world. He said he had sufficient clout with the Egyptian authorities to be able to obtain a scholarship for me to study there. He saw his department taking a lead in that area and introducing Arabic studies at the University of Cameroon in Yaounde.

My decision to take a totally different route in life laid waste all those plans he was beginning to nurture for me in his department. As we talked, he said something quite poignant when he asked me to look at him. "I am no longer a young man," he said, "and I don't have long to be here at the University. I'll really be happy if you are on my staff before I finally retire." Looking at him and seeing how helpless he looked, I felt a lump crawling up my throat and the confusion I thought I had laid to rest, bounced back. Before me that morning, Professor Fonlon suddenly appeared frail, weak, old and frustrated. My heart nearly missed a beat. I told him I would think about it.

When I left his office, I went back to Professor Lantum's office to give him an account of our meeting, which had further intensified my confusion. Should I go, or should I not go? Professor Lantum left his desk, walked up to me, placed his hand on my shoulder, looked at me in the eye and said: "Don't miss this opportunity to leave this country. It is not always easy for anyone to leave but now that it is the Presidency itself asking you to go, go without delay! Don't look back! Just Go! If you get there and things don't work out for you, you can always switch fields and do whatever you want. But, for heavens' sake, don't stay! Go!"

I did not know if he realised how helpful his words were to me. I walked out of his office and went straight to my friend and brother, John B's house in the Melen neighbourhood, to tell him I was leaving. Professor Lantum had assured me he would talk to my brother about my sudden departure and that he would understand and so would the rest of the family. I still had one difficult step to take, though: go back to Professor Fonlon and tell him I had weighed his offer carefully but would not be taking it. And that is what I did the next day. I thanked him for his confidence in me but said I was leaving all the same. He seemed shattered by my decision but said he understood and wished me well.

From Professor Fonlon's office, I took a taxi to the Cameroon Airlines office where I booked a flight for Madrid. I met a surprisingly polite and jovial young man in his early twenties, who attended to me. He insisted on speaking to me in English but soon gave up, complaining that English was a difficult language. As he and I were talking, a young woman walked in, stood by me at the counter for a few minutes and then asked if my name was Martin. The answer being affirmative, she said she was Solange and that she too was going to Madrid. She had been told about me at the Presidency but she could not pin a face on my name. But when she heard us discussing about the flight to Madrid, she guessed who I was. I said I too was glad to meet her. I recalled seeing her from a distance in one or two of the classes we had in common with our francophone counterparts. Merely seeing her and knowing that we were heading for the same destination gave me some comfort.

As we talked, the young man booking our flight, asked us to smuggle him along in our luggage. We all laughed and he said even though he worked for the airline company, he had never had a chance to fly before. He certainly had a sense of humour, which was a far cry from our typical Cameroonian civil servant, who is reputed for rudeness. Even though Solange and I were to travel on the same flight, we were to part ways in Paris as she had family she wanted to visit before flying to Madrid at a later date. I was only to be in Paris long enough to transit to the Spanish carrier, Iberian, later the same day.

On the morning of my departure, I asked the taxi driver taking me to the airport to stop over at my friend John B's house. He had told me he would like to accompany me to the airport. As we were about to leave, he gave me a fur-coated jacket that was to save me from the Madrid cold that winter. I was leaving Cameroon at the onset of winter in Europe totally unprepared for it. Had he not given me that fur-coated jacket, I would have had it rough in Madrid.

Several years later, John was to remind me of that day I left for Madrid, drenched in tears. We were sitting in my office in Douala where I worked for an American oil company. John always dropped by whenever he was in transit through Douala, especially when he worked for the International Criminal Tribunal for Rwanda in Arusha, Tanzania. He recalled that as he stood at the airport watching as I boarded the plane, he suddenly saw someone racing across the tarmac to the plane. To his surprise, it was Professor Lantum. He wondered where the professor was going and why he was boarding the plane just as it was about to taxi down the runway. Inside the plane, I did not know what was happening outside but I recalled that as the plane was about to leave, I suddenly heard someone calling my name. I turned round and it was Professor Lantum coming towards me. He handed me an envelope, wished me well and disappeared. I was so stunned that I did not know what to do or say. As the plane taxied down the runway ready for take-off, I opened the envelope and it contained the sum of a hundred thousand francs CFA. I wept openly for I had practically no money on me, counting only on the stipend I was told would be waiting for me on arrival in Madrid.

I remember arriving at the Barajas International Airport and, after the usual security clearance, I walked out into a bitingly cold windy September evening, and I was glad I had the fur-coated jacket John B had given me earlier in the day. From Paris to Madrid, I had been musing over the Spanish I knew and wondering if I was ever going to understand the language, or to be understood in turn. I was right to be worried because, no sooner had I arrived than I was faced with the frustrations that come from not being able to understand or speak a language.

The first thing I did was to go up to a policeman who was standing nearby to ask for directions. I stood there speechless as the man babbled away like a machine gun. The blank expression on my face said it all and he just burst into laughter, shrugged his shoulders and walked away. Then I saw a rent-a-car office not far from there. I knew that one of the young women I saw there would at least speak English or French, and I was right. One of them spoke impeccable English and I told her I was just coming in and that I did not speak Spanish at all. Could she get me a cab that would drop me in a reasonably cheap hotel as I did not have much money on me? I also told her to let me know how much such a ride would cost as I was still not familiar with the Spanish currency, the 'Peseta'. She did just that and I spent my first night in Madrid in a clean, reasonably affordable hotel.

The day after my arrival in Madrid, I went to the Spanish foreign ministry as an official at their embassy in Yaounde had instructed me to do. To my utter despair, I was told that my file had not yet arrived from their embassy in Yaounde, and so they could not pay my stipend. In a panic, I went to our embassy to find out if there was a way they could help expedite the process from Yaounde by asking the Linguistics Services of the Presidency to intervene with the Spanish embassy to speed matters up.

If they had politely told me there was not much they could do from their end, I would have understood and appreciated their response. Instead, the rude workers started making fun of me, calling me a liar and an adventurer who had missed his way into the embassy and was trying to scam them into believing that he was a bona fide student on the pay of the Spanish government. I stormed out of there in a murderous rage and vowed never to step my foot in that office again.

As I stood on the pavement wondering which way to go, a young man I had seen sitting in one office at the embassy, came out of the building and walked towards me, a smile on his face. Someone from the embassy smiling? I was wary of him as he came up to me. He said his name was Pierre; what was mine? I told him my name and he asked me where I was from. "From Cameroon, why?" I asked, not sure where he was leading.

"No, I know you're from Cameroon, but from what part, what

tribe?" Each time anyone asks me about my tribe, I always feel something bad is about to happen. I told him I was a Cameroonian, period. But he was not one to be dissuaded so easily because he insisted to know. I scrutinised his face closely to see what he was up to and seeing that he did not seem to mean any harm, I said:

"Since you insist, I come from Nsoland in the northwest province."

"Je savais, je savais qu'on était des frères. Oui, on est des frères, toi et moi!" he shouted, hugging me.

"How are we brothers?" I asked, truly intrigued and feeling a little embarrassed as he was hugging me and laughing loud. Heads were already turning towards us and I saw question marks in many eyes.

"Je suis Bamoun de Foumban, moi. Tu es Banso. Donc, on est des frères, non?"

Yes, he was right. The Bamun and my people of Nsoland, trace their origin to the same Tikar ancestry. Geographically, we live side-by-side, being separated only by a small stream. Historically, colonialism put us apart, the Bamun having been colonised by the French while my people had fallen into the hands of the British after World War One. Before the British and the French, we were under the German yoke until Germany lost World War One and the victors, the British and the French tore us apart.

For once, tribalism seemed to be working in my favour. I asked where he was studying and he told me he was not a student. He was an artist, painting portraits of people in the Madrid subway for a living. I wondered if that was enough to bring in a substantial income to survive in Madrid. For an answer, he merely pouted his lips and said, *"Oui, ça va, ça va. Je me débrouille pas mal."* We were now sitting in a small café on one of the streets some distance away from the embassy. I asked how he had found his way to Madrid. He said he had come to Madrid five years earlier through northern Nigeria, to Niger and to Morocco before crossing the Mediterranean Sea into Spain from the Spanish North African autonomous city of Ceuta near Morocco.

"Dis-donc, à l'ambassade on m'appelle un aventurier, alors que c'est toi le vrai aventurier, Pierre," I said. He gave a full-throated laugh

and said those fellows at the embassy were mere rogues. His brother worked there but everyone else there was just a moron, he said. He then took me to a relatively inexpensive hostel where he was staying where I also got a room for a few months. He and I became good friends but he was someone on the move and, before long, he left for Barcelona and that was the last I heard of him.

A month later, someone called me from our embassy to let me know that the Spanish Foreign Office had sent documents for the ambassador's signature and that I should stop by and pick them up. I arrived a little unsure of what was waiting for me. I hoped that the encounter that morning would be a more cordial one, but I was wrong. One official saw me and exclaimed, to everyone's hearing, *"L'aventurier là est encore ici?"* I snapped back that I was not an '*aventurier*' and that the only thing that had brought me to the embassy was to collect some documents which they should have signed for me.

As it is typical of Cameroonian high-ranking officials in the civil service, he asked me if I knew who I was talking to. I said I did not but that I was there only to collect my documents. He said I was being impolite; that he had seen my type throughout Europe and that he had been told that I was an anglophone and that, like all 'anglos', I was surely an opponent of our government. He then added that I was going to gain nothing by bullying my way around, and that I still had a long way to go and some hard lessons to learn.

I decided that the best thing to do was to get out of there so as not to say something nasty to him, which was not my intention. I had nothing to gain by that; instead I knew that I would have much to lose through such a confrontation. As I was about to leave, a kind-hearted secretary told me that my document had been signed but that the ambassador was at a meeting outside the embassy and all the documents he had signed before leaving were still in his office. She suggested that I come back the next day.

Early the next day, I arrived and sat waiting in the lounge. Shortly thereafter, a young, eye-catching girl walked in and took a seat opposite me. She greeted me and reached out for a newspaper that was on the table. She must have noticed how my roaming eyes were boring holes into her. She then decided to make the best of it by burying her eyes in the paper but occasionally crossing and crisscrossing her legs, the better for me to see whatever it was I was so eager to see. Oh, that smooth highway to perdition! That cat-and-mouse game went on for a while before a man suddenly burst through the door. It was the same chap with whom I had exchanged harsh words a few days earlier. When he saw us together, he started screaming at the top of his voice and ordering the girl to leave immediately.

He then sat down opposite me, stared at me sternly in the eye and said, almost without opening his lips, that he was going to wring my neck, and as he spoke, he twisted some paper he had in his hand to show me how my neck would look like if I was nursing any lecherous interest in his daughter. We sat for a minute in silence, sizing each other up and I stared him directly in the eye, and asked why he did not keep his daughter locked up in a cage at home. For a second, I thought he was going to punch me in the face. I saw him clench his fist menacingly letting a growl escape from his lips. Then he dropped his fist, stood up and continued to stare down at me. I also stood up, not being sure what his intentions were. We continued to size each other up and before walking out the door, he stopped, turned round and told me that we anglophones were Cameroon's true problems. I burst out laughing and he, looking quite confused, said he knew we were eternally disgruntled people, who were out to wreak havoc in our country. "If you think you can bring disorder here at the embassy, think again, my friend. You will not succeed." With that, he slammed the door behind him.

He succeeded to turn the whole embassy staff against me, accusing me, in particular, and anglophones, in general, of never being satisfied with anything. It was from him that I heard the expression *"les aigris eternels"* ('an eternally disgruntled lot'). He also warned whoever would listen to be careful with me, calling me a dangerous fellow to watch around anyone's wife or daughter. *"L'anglo là est dangereux; c'est un pervers sexuel, attention avec lui!"* Needless to say that I left without my documents.

When I left the embassy that morning in a fit of rage, I decided to take a stroll down a broad avenue to a public park not far away. There I sat, watching people going about their lives. Three-piece-suited men, with heavy briefcases in hand, walked to or from a bank opposite the street. I imagined those briefcases being stuffed with cash while I sat there not sure of where I would get a few pesetas for lunch. In the see-through office windows, slim, elegant, high-heel-shod women sat over typewriters, or talked on the phone, or walked elegantly around with folders in their hands. There were men, some in suits, others with long-sleeve shirts and ties on their necks, poring over files, looking so amazingly at ease with themselves and with the world around them. There I was, alone and dejected, listening to my intestines growling and complaining in the grips of hunger while the rest of business Madrid drifted peacefully past.

I did not seem to be alone in my misery, though. There were other drifters too, who stood idly by, alone or in small groups, loitering aimlessly about, hands in their pockets, noses in the air from which cigarette smoke bellowed as from chimneys. Some lay snoring on nearby benches, while others just sat there, visibly doped. A few even bumped me for a peseta but when I lifted my empty hands in the air, they wished me well and drifted away. Misery brought our worlds together. They made me think, "You're not alone in this unfair world, old boy!" And I even took some comfort in that feeling.

Then I noticed at one corner the gigantic statue of the skinny Don Quijote de la Mancha on his skeletal horse. I went near and was struck by its sheer size, gigantic as it truly was. We were then reading the famous Spanish tale of the same name, *Don Quijote de la Mancha*, in one of our Spanish literature classes. And there he was, Don Quijote de la Mancha, apparently preparing an assault against some invisible windmills which might have appeared to him like devils, while his pot-bellied servant, Sancho, stared on abashed. Miguel Cervantes, the author, certainly churned out a strange character, who designated a girl in a neighbouring farm the love of his life without the girl ever knowing about it. He then renamed her *Dulcinea del Toboso* and went on what he believed were adventures of chivalry that would enable him to conquer the world, and make it a safe place for him to marry her and they would live happily there ever after.

Our literature professor loved that tale. She was already a woman of a certain age but still head-turningly attractive, and always elegantly dressed. She was said to be of Spanish nobility and always wore heavy make-up and a bright-red lipstick that covered her entire lips which she pouted seductively as she spoke. She had an easy smile which revealed a set of uniform white teeth and she seemed quite conscious of the effect her movements and facial expressions had on some of us, especially the male students. She had a pure Madrilenian accent to match, and it was always a delight to listen to her read lengthy passages from *Don Quijote*, varying the tone of her voice to perfectly capture the scene she was reading. According to her, there was no other work of literature anywhere in the world that matched that masterpiece of Spanish literature. She insisted on calling the book by its lengthy title: "*El ingenioso caballero Don Quijote de la Mancha.*"

As I sauntered about aimlessly, I ran into other statues of well-known men and women of Spanish literature and culture. I seemed to be standing in the middle of the Madrid of poetic ecstasy with poets of renown staring at me. I could recognize a few, mainly those we were studying in class: Antonio Machado, Federico Lorca, Unamuno, among others. Somewhere along my way, I ran into the Madrid of classical music with Pablo Cassals, the outstanding Spanish cellist some critics consider the pre-eminent cellist of the first half of the 20th century, and one of the greatest cellists of all times. Then there were the great painters: Pablo Ruiz Picasso and Salvador Dali. Around each of those statues, water fountains spurted magnificent successive jets of water into the air. Piercing through those jets of water, as they rose and fell in rapid successions, were beams of light that turned and twisted, bathing the sprinting water in a rainbow of magnificent colours. When I finally decided to walk back home, the anger that had been suffocating me when I left our embassy was gone; even the hunger that had been gnawing away at my entrails had felt sorry for me and left me alone. Even though I was a long way from my apartment, I still decided to cover the distance on foot.

***

When I came back home from our embassy, I wrote a letter dripping with frustration to Professor Lantum, wondering aloud if my departure for Spain had been such a bright idea after all. I told him how the Spanish government and our embassy had combined to frustrate my stay in Madrid. I told him how practically broke I was, and how desperate and totally frustrated I was feeling. I must have sounded suicidal because Professor Lantum sent me a magnificent reply to my letter that brought me back to my senses and made me face the reality of the life I was then living. He delved into Nso martial history, reminding me that we, Nso people, have always been fighters from time immemorial; that no Nso man worth the name ever fled from the battlefield, and that every Nso man, who has ever fallen in battle, did so with a spear sticking out of his chest, never out of his back. Only cowards, in their flight from the carnage of the battlefield, received the spear in their back, not a true son of Nso soil. He said having worked with me, he knew that I was no coward and that I could and would overcome whatever obstacles there were on my path. Those were mere temporary problems of money and adjustment to a new culture and he knew I would overcome them. He literally ordered me to stop whining and groaning like a kid and lift myself off the gutter of despair into which I was sinking. Where, on God's good earth, had a Nso man, worth the name, ever been known to shed tears? Tears were for women and children, not for men, and that I should not forget that I was now a man!

I had never received a much more heart-warming letter than that before, nor have I received any ever since then. It lifted me from the gutter of despair to the real life around me, and, poor as I remained for a good part of the first months in Madrid, I never again questioned the wisdom of my presence in the Spanish capital. In fact, I even started laughing my troubles away. I just did not focus on poverty or loneliness anymore. I had a definite purpose in mind, which was to study the language and head out for greater pursuits. Surprisingly, as I began to realise that I could not change the world to fit my changing moods, I started to focus on changing my moods to fit the world I was living in. No amount of kicking and screaming was going to make the Spaniards pay my stipend sooner, so I decided not to make the non-payment of the said stipend an issue for a court case, and, with my mind focused on other things, I began to enjoy my studies.

Professor Daniel Noni Lantum: He gave me my first job and paid my first salary in 1975

I even began to make friends with Spanish and foreign students alike. I even received a proposal from one student to move into an apartment much closer to the university, which he was sharing with four other students, and I was only too happy to comply. We called it *"las Naciones Unidas"*, the "United Nations", because we came from different countries of the world. One fellow was from the United States, representing North America, another from Peru, representing South America, one from Japan, representing Asia, I was from Cameroon, representing the great continent of Africa. We also had a Spanish guy with us, home bred and proud of his historic city, Madrid. To him, Madrid was the centre of the universe. Was it not from Madrid, then the centre of civilised humanity, that the great conquistadores had fanned out into the world, subduing it and planting the Spanish royal flag in remote corners of the world, especially in the Americas? *"Viva, Espana!"* he would scream, punching the air with his fist. What a great chap Pasqua was!

Life became fun as we would buy bottles of excellent Spanish wine and chill out in the living room in the evening, listening to Spanish flamenco dance music oozing out of the turntable at the corner. Before Professor Lantum's letter, I was a grouchy and sullen man and none of the students with me in class dared approach me, which increased my feeling of despair and loneliness. After his letter, I took control of my life, changed my focus to more productive pursuits and Madrid became a marvellous city for me. I did not suddenly become rich, but I ceased thinking of myself as a poor helpless African student, waiting cap in hand for a handout. I no longer vented my bile on whoever happened to be near me, or whoever asked an innocent question about my country, as many did so often. The radical change of my moods for the better came as a result of Professor Lantum's robust reminder to me that I needed to lift myself out of that complaining phase and go on with my life. In the face of adversity, he warned, chickening out was not the solution. Focusing my attention and energy on what really mattered was what I needed to do, and he was right.

***

At last, I received my stipend from the Spanish foreign ministry just on time to accompany the American student I shared the apartment with and his class on a tour of Spain. He was in a different school and when he mentioned that their class was taking a trip around Spain, I thought it was a good idea. I asked if I too could accompany them. He said he would ask the organisers of the tour. He came back the next day and said it was fine with them. All I needed to do was pay the fee and I was welcome aboard. It turned out to be one of the best decisions I ever made during the one year I was in Madrid. We travelled northwards towards the Basque country but avoided to go closer as that territory was still in open rebellion against the central government in Madrid, and attacks on tourists was not a rarity. We visited important historical sites and monuments among which was the city of Santiago de Compostela, the capital of the region of Galicia. What took us there was the famous 'Camino de Santiago', the pilgrimage route and the cathedral in which the remains of the Apostle James are said to lie buried. From there, we visited the small coastal town of El Ferrol at the north-eastern tip of Spain, the birthplace of the Spanish dictator, *El Generalisimo* Francisco Franco, who adopted the title of *"El Caudillo,"* meaning "The Leader". He ruled Spain with an iron fist from 1939 until his death in 1975, a year before I arrived in Madrid.

We skirted the Portuguese borders to the west, often stopping to watch cities in Portugal only a few miles away. Since I did not have a Portuguese visa, we decided not to make a quick trip to one of those small towns, attractive though that option sounded. Americans and Spaniards with me would have had no problems crossing over there, but I was the only one who needed a visa to cross the border. Other memorable places we visited were in the southern regions of Spain that had been under Muslim domination for over eight centuries. We were then studying Spanish history and it was great to visit some of the historic sites I heard about in my class, especially the region of Andalusia. At the height of their conquest of Spain, the Moors from North Africa had established what came to be known as the Caliphate of Cordoba that covered most of the Iberian Peninsula, which included huge chunks of Portugal, Spain and even southern France.

We visited numerous remnants of the Moorish rule, particularly the numerous castles strewn all over southern Spain.

* * *

Beside Solange, there was one other Cameroonian student, a young man called Denis, who was with us in the same programme. Both Solange and Denis were French-speaking. Solange, as mentioned earlier, had been with me in the bilingual programme at the University of Yaoundé while Denis was from the Higher Teacher Training College, more commonly known by its French appellation, *Ecole Normale Supérieure*. Solange had the advantage of being from the same ethnic group that dominated the embassy staff. When we arrived in Madrid, the embassy rented a house outside the city for all of us. We each had our individual rooms and life during the first few months was not too bad. I hated the distance from the university, which was nearly an hour of changing buses and subways that became quite infernal during morning or evening rush hours.

My relationship with my two colleagues was quite cordial even at the height of my rocky relationship with some of the embassy officials. Solange remained a good friend even when I left our common apartment to move closer to the university. She took the same courses with me and kept me constantly abreast of events at the embassy, all the gossips especially those at my expense, which seemed to have been many. Denis, who was from the western part of the country, and who was also largely distrusted at the embassy, did somehow gain their trust and confidence mainly at my expense. I was only too happy to distance myself from him. Shortly after I moved out of our apartment, Solange also left and took a room closer to the university, sharing it with some French girls.

As soon as the school year was over, Solange and I went to the French embassy and applied for visas for France. The visas granted, I left for Paris, leaving her behind in Madrid. Our paths crossed again some months later in Paris, where we wrote the test into the Ecole

Supérieure d'Interprétariat et de Traduction (ESIT). She was successful and I was not. After the test, one of the teachers came to me, congratulated me on my efforts in the test but thought that my background in English studies prepared me better for a school in England or America, which was a very polite way of saying I had flunked the test.

I was wondering what to do next, when Solange came looking for me a few days later to tell me that she had gone to our country's embassy in Paris and one official had advised that I enrol in a French programme pending my transfer to an English school of translation and interpretation by year's end. Needless to say that the embassy was staffed by people from her ethnic group, who kept her informed of what to do. I deeply appreciated her help in those moments of anguish in the French capital. Thanks to her, I was able to receive a hearing at the embassy and my stipend was paid with no difficulty. I registered in a Master's degree programme in African studies at the University of Paris III, Sorbonne Nouvelle.

In Paris, I benefitted from the generosity of some people I had heard about in the past but had never met before. Two of them are worth mentioning as we have remained friends since. Henry Bongasu Kishani was then enrolled in a doctoral programme at the Sorbonne. He opened the door of his room at the Cité Universitaire to me for the first few months before I moved to a small room of my own. He is a good poet and has had many collections of poems to his credit. There was Augustine Santeh who was in a French language immersion programme in a nearby school. He was there a year or two before I arrived, and he and I trudged the streets of Paris together and shared many a meagre meal either in his room or in mine.

Life in Paris turned out to be quite tough, especially as all I could afford as room and board was a tiny room with a dirty-rugged floor, with faded-papered walls and a rusty, iron-barred window on the seventh floor of an old building - commonly called *"la chambre de bonne."* There was no shower; just a rust-eaten tap from which water of undetermined colour dripped perpetually into a small sink, polished by countless scars from who could tell how many numerous fingers? There was no lift either, just an age-blackened, spiralling staircase, lit by a rheumatic light bulb that dimly illuminated walls that were glistening with the sweat of open, unflushed nearby toilets. I stepped out onto the sludge-covered sidewalks one winter morning on my way to the bus stop when I felt water seeping into the sole of my only pair of shoes. I went back to my room, took off the shoes and the socks that were all dripping wet and had to wait home all day for the socks and the shoes to dry. With nothing to eat in my room, I was forced to sit listening to my intestines grumbling and churning in the grips of hunger.

Not all was gloomy in Paris, though. I did pick up a job as a delivery driver for a few months, picking up goods from a warehouse in the suburbs for the main store in the city. With the income from that job, I was able to keep a good supply of food in the cupboard which I gracefully shared with Augustine whenever he came visiting, which was often since he lived less than a mile down the road. It was in Paris that I intensified my writing efforts. I had begun writing in Madrid just to keep myself busy, especially in those moments when the city was in the grips of a biting cold wind that blew from the Sahara Desert across the Mediterranean.

When I arrived in Paris and discovered that Henry Bongasu Kishani was already a consummate poet, I showed him the few things I had written myself and received valuable words of encouragement from him. I even tried my hand on a short play which I intended to enter for a competition organised by the Africa Service of the British Broadcasting Corporation (BBC) in London. During my last year at the Federal Bilingual Grammar School in Buea in 1970, I had entered a similar BBC poetry competition and one of my poems had been selected and read on the air. My English teacher, a certain Mr. Miller, an English man, had praised my efforts to the hearing of my classmates, which constituted quite an ego-boosting moment for me. From thence forward, I was determined to be a writer, just as my brother Kenjo was. The urge to write surged in Paris and I churned out quite a mix of poetry, short plays and short stories.

Years later, when I read some of the poems I had written in Paris, I was stunned by the dark images that my mind had belched. It was just a bunch of withered images, twirling in despair, coiling in uncertainty and recoiling in the froth of beer. I could not find that proverbial beauty for which Paris is so famous, especially in spring when metaphors, similes, and euphemisms are rumoured to waltz jubilantly on the mirthful tongues of poets. I could not find the overwhelming beauty of Paris many a poet sang so noisily about. In vain, I searched for the Paris where romantic tales are said to twirl off the nibs of writers' pens like smoke from abandoned, ash-trayed cigarettes in noisy cafés; the Paris where the brush in artists' discoloured fingers are said to rainbow the hopes of mankind on canvas! Why did the legendary beauty of Paris disappear in my presence?

***

One of the best decisions I made in Paris was to learn to type, a skill I would later benefit from immensely. Henry, who had learnt to type when he was in a Catholic seminary in Rome, told me that if I ever wanted to be a writer, I necessarily had to learn to type whatever I wrote myself. "You learn to edit your work yourself as you type it," he told me. My university encouraged students to learn to type for a small fee so they could type their own theses themselves. There was a big room for that purpose, fully equipped with typewriters with instructors at hand to guide the students. I heeded Henry's advice and parted with my hard-earned cash to learn to type instead of drowning it in wine or beer. My typing skill enabled me to type my own creative work myself instead of scribbling it on pieces of paper that I left floating around my room. The wisdom of that decision has followed me all my life.

It was also in Paris that I became a blood donor. I did not go out looking for the Red Cross to donate my blood. It happened quite unexpectedly. A Cameroonian friend of mine and I left our morning class one day and were heading for the underground train station, when we saw, parked by the roadside, a bus bearing the unmistakable emblem of the Red Cross. I could see quite some movement inside and around it.

We could have passed by without a second glance had a certain elegantly and smartly dressed, medium height woman, of a certain age already, wearing a smile that covered her face from ear to ear, not stopped us and invited us to donate our blood. Her request took me completely aback and, without much reflection on my part, I asked her if they also wanted blood from people like my friend and me. I had not sincerely thought that the French Red Cross would want blood from black people. It is incredible how much racism you assimilate when you live in a society where you feel the dividing line between the races so acutely.

That spunky old woman, who still had a lot of life in her, suddenly spun round to face me. The smile had gone from her face and she grabbed me by the arm, looked at me directly in the eye and said: "My son, why do you young people continue to promote this obnoxious exclusiveness. Aren't we all human beings? Does the blood that flow through your veins have a different colour from the one that flows through mine? Please, my son, refrain from promoting this division among us. If you don't feel like giving your blood, I understand, but it shouldn't be for the reason you evoke here."

I was taken completely aback by her reaction. I had expected her to turn her back on us and go for the other people of her colour but there she was taking the time to remind me of the oneness of humanity, and how narrow my own understanding of that humanity was! As I listened to her, I suddenly remembered my sister, Monica, who died some years before. She would, however, have died several years earlier had some people, many unknown to us, not given her their blood.

I was still very young then when she took ill and was rushed to the Catholic Hospital in Shisong. She was in hospital for several weeks when one day my parents appeared extremely worried. I could hear them in hushed tones discussing my sister's illness and, from every indication, all was not well. Then my father called my brother,

Denis, and me and asked us to walk the ten miles that separated the hospital at Shisong from our home to give some food to our sister and to greet her.

We were always excited when we had to travel out of our village of Nkar to Kumbo or Shisong. We loved the open spaces and the fresh air and the hills that roll on and on like waves and the valleys we had to cross to reach our destination. A journey on foot of about three hours would take us nearly twice as long.

When we arrived at the hospital, we saw the doctors and the nurses in their impeccably white garments, with stethoscopes around their necks. We admired the clinically clean environment of the hospital although I immediately hated, as I still do, the all-pervasive smell of the drugs that always wafts through hospital wards. I have always found something inexplicably intimidating about hospitals, perhaps the fear of death which I always associate with them. That was perhaps one reason I never ever dreamt of studying medicine. Even when friends of mine and I discussed future careers, medicine was never on my list.

When we were shown the ward where our sister was, we met a cousin of ours sitting on one of the benches in the hospital courtyard. He immediately led us into our sister's ward. What struck me then, and I still occasionally have visions of that scene, was the sight of a small plastic bag with a red liquid in it hanging over my sister's bed. From it, a tube led out and buried itself into her arm. I could not believe what I was seeing. And was that frail figure in bed really my sister, who was always plumb-looking? It was only when she turned round, saw us and rewarded our presence with a smile that I saw that it was really her. A lump immediately rushed up my throat and my eyes instantly clouded with tears. My sister could barely speak and seemed to be in considerable pain. Shortly thereafter, two nurses walked in, gave us broad smiles and asked us to step out of the room while they attended to our sister.

As we stood speechless outside, our cousin told us of people donating blood to our sister, and invited us to go and see for ourselves. We followed him down the long, impeccably clean corridor, reeking with drugs of all sorts. From an open window, we saw an uncle of ours and two other people lying propped up on beds, with tubes dangling from their arms and emptying blood into little pocket-like containers. Our uncle called out to us and told us he was giving blood for our sister. He then pointed to the other two men with him and asked us to greet them because they too had volunteered to give her blood.

I did not then understand what giving blood to someone really meant. My attention was entirely focused on those needles sticking out of their arms and I remember wincing from the imaginary pain I thought they must be feeling. Oh, that much blood being drained from someone's arm! I did not think I could give away so much blood and still be alive! That scene of people sitting there with their arms stretched out and needles sticking from them was to remain with me for several years to come.

Our cousin then told us that those generous people were just passers-by when they were asked to kindly donate their blood to save our sister. They had voluntarily agreed to help even though they did not know who she was. How selfless and generous they were! Our sister pulled through that crisis and recovered well enough to come back home to us.

I remember how she always thanked those people who had been so generous with their blood that gave her a new lease of life. She did not even know what was happening as she had drifted in and out of consciousness the whole time, but whenever she talked about her stay in hospital, which was quite often, she always recalled the huge quantity of blood that she received. "And where would so much blood have come from, had it not been for some generous souls?" she always wondered.

Several decades later, there I was in Paris, of all places, faced with the decision to either give my own blood to save someone else's life, as some had done to save my sister's, or turn around and go my way. I thought of the biblical story of the good Samaritan who, unlike the priest and the Levite, had refused to walk on the other side of the road, choosing instead to come to the rescue of a battered Jew, his traditional enemy. It was then that I opted to say 'YES!' to life by cooperating with the Red Cross. As the lively old lady showed us where to go, I thought I saw my sister, Monica's face at one corner of the sky, nodding her head approvingly and urging me to give my blood. And I did. I walked up into that bus and my Cameroonian friend, after much hesitation, also followed. We were greeted by nurses, men and women, dressed in impeccably white gowns, whose reassuring greetings and smiles drove away the fear we had of parting with our blood. When we told them it was the first time each of us was donating blood, one of the nurses put a reassuring hand on my shoulder and commended us for our great gesture that would surely save a life. We were told not to worry as it would be over before we knew it. I felt a slight pain as the syringe homed into my vein and I was told to relax my fist and let the blood ooze down feely into the tube and into a small container beside me.

Twenty minutes, or so later, it was over and we were given a cup of warm milk with a piece of bread and then released with many thanks from the nurses. At the foot of the bus, stood the grandmother, who had rebuked me for my comment earlier. She walked up to us and surprised us with big kisses on our cheeks. I walked away happy that I had achieved something great that day. To my Cameroonian friend, it was just one of those adventures one falls into during one's stay in Europe. To me, however, it was the beginning of what has become a regular exercise I perform for my sister, Monica. Each time I give my blood, I see her there at the corner of my mind, smiling approvingly and I know that I'm doing the right thing.

The Paris Red Cross later sent us certificates as blood donors. I proudly carried mine with me for a good number of years thereafter. In all countries I have been to, I have always been generous with my blood, and no one has ever turned it down because it comes from a black man.

**

It was in Paris that, for the first time, I met African writers and writers of African descent in the diaspora. The first was the prolific Congolese poet, playwright and novelist, Tchicaya U'tamsi. It came at a time of particularly intense literary effervescence in Africa where the proponents and opponents of such concepts as "Négritude," "African Personality," "Métissage culturel," among others, were daily clashing in literary arenas. The names of Leopold Sedar Senghor, Senegalese poet and statesman, Léon Gontran Damas of French Guyana, and Aimé Césaire of the French island of Martinique, the latter being a deputy in the French National Assembly, floated in the air wherever there was a gathering of students of African literature. The Senghor-Césaire-Damas trio was largely credited with the creation of the controversial concept of 'Negritude,' which aimed at raising awareness of "black consciousness" across Africa and its diaspora. To further muddy the already turbid waters of the African literary spring, Nigeria's Wole Soyinka, who would later receive the Nobel Prize in Literature, being the first African writer to be so honoured, let drop another problematical concept, which he dubbed 'Tigritude'. Many saw it as a deliberate attempt to counter and ridicule the philosophy behind 'Négritude' with its near-obsessional emphasis on being of black African origin. "Does a tiger stand in the forest and announce, 'I am a tiger'? No," proclaimed the coiner of that concept, Wole Soyinka. "A tiger does not proclaim its *tigritude*, it pounces."

It was during that period of confusion on the African literary scene that Tchicaya U'tamsi was invited to Paris III, Sorbonne Nouvelle, where I was studying. On that day, Tchicaya faced an unsympathetic audience, especially the younger generation that was very vocal in its rejection of the concept of 'Negritude'. He began by openly declaring that he was just an African writer and that labels did not mean much to him. That did not seem to impress some very loud young critics. One of them in particular was from the West African nation of Dahomey, that had been renamed Benin. That tiny West African nation saw one coup d'état after another in rapid succession as army generals wrestled for power. At the time of our meeting with Tchicaya, another low-ranking army man had just seized power, propelled himself to rank of "Army General and Supreme Leader of the Nation" and declared Marxism-Leninism to be the ideology that would lead his people to political and economic salvation. One of its enthusiastic supporters was the fellow who loudly opposed Tchicaya that morning, dismissing his impressive literary output as sheer 'bourgeois nonsense'. When some of us expressed alarm at his views and objected to such insulting language, the fiery Marxist-Leninist stormed out of the hall, loudly denouncing all of us as *"les lèches culs de l'impérialisme yanqui'* (ass-lickers of Yankee imperialism).

In the midst of all that turmoil, Tchicaya remained unfazed, keeping a smile on his face. When all was calm, he spoke in a gentle voice, loudly appealing for tolerance and respect of others' views, even if we did not share them. He strongly defended artistic freedom, denied that his work was hermetic and invited critics to penetrate his literary creation through the doors of black history. He received a standing ovation when he had spoken. He left a good impression on me.

CHAPTER 12

AMERICA, HERE I COME! - 1978

I came back home one evening and the janitor of the building, a nice gentleman of Moroccan origin, who always called me '*mon cher frère camerounais*', told me my landlady, Madame De Lavalle, wanted to see me. She lived in a huge mansion about a mile away. She proudly traced her ancestry to the French nobility of old, and spoke French with Parisian elegance. When I knocked, I was surprised it was her who opened the door for me and held it open until I walked in. She wore a broad smile and I could see slight cracks on the thick rouge on her lips. She seemed to be floating in a thick fume of nose-tickling aroma which seemed to cling, not only on her person, but also onto everything else around the house. I could still smell some of it on my body for the entire week thereafter.

As I sat wondering what it was all about, she picked up a small piece of paper from a side table with a telephone number on it. She told me she had received a call from the American embassy asking me to call as soon as possible. I was stunned because I knew no one at the American embassy and could not figure out who could want to see me there and why. I did not even know where it was located. She knew where it was and wrote the address down for me on that same piece of paper. I thanked her and left. I went directly to a pay phone, called the number I was given and told the woman at the other end that the embassy had called me and I was just wondering what it was for.

She asked for my name and then invited me to come to the embassy the next day at 10 o'clock. What was it about? She said it was about studying translation and interpretation in the United States, and that I should come with all my certificates and my passport.

The next day, I rang the doorbell to the American embassy and after a minute or two, a neatly dressed army officer opened and asked if he could help me. I told him I had spoken to a lady the previous day, who had asked me to bring my certificates and passport for studies in the US. He then picked up the phone, spoke to someone out of sight and then ushered me in. At the front desk, a young lady welcomed me with a smile and asked for my passport and accompanying documents. She asked me to take a seat. She took my certificates and passport to another room, came back a few minutes later with a folder in hand, and asked me to follow her. She led the way up a flight of stairs and knocked on one of the doors. A voice answered and she opened the door for me to go in. She announced my presence and handed the folder she had to a middle-aged man in a long-sleeve shirt and a tie sitting behind a big nicely polished desk. He greeted me and motioned me to a chair facing his desk. He opened the folder that had just been placed before him, glanced through it for a minute, put it aside and said my academic credentials were impressive.

He then told me that there was an agreement between the United States government and my country's government for a scholarship he called the "Ahidjo-Kennedy Scholarship" that would enable me to study translation and interpretation at Georgetown University in Washington, DC. He asked if I had heard of Georgetown and I told him I knew many translators and interpreters from Cameroon who had studied there. He said Georgetown was a good school and hoped I would enjoy my studies there. We talked some more and I learnt that he had worked at the US embassy in Yaounde some years earlier. His duties had enabled him to cover all the countries of the Central African region. Before long, we were discussing African history, politics, and academics as if we had been friends for long. He then bade me goodbye and good luck with my studies. I thanked him and took the stairs down to the secretariat where the secretary asked me to pick up my passport and air-ticket the next day. I thanked her and walked out into a bright sunny summer day in August. It was one of the few times during my stay in Paris that I found that city unbelievably calm, peaceful and gentle to me.

* * *

I flew into Dulles International Airport in Washington, DC, one humid August afternoon. When I went through immigration, I walked to the sliding door leading out of the airport. The heat from outside caught me in the face with unexpected suddenness. It was as if a lid of a pot with boiling water had just been opened in my face. I remember jumping back into the air-conditioned waiting room. A gentleman, who was following me, saw my instinctive reaction and burst out laughing. "Welcome to Washington, DC, Sir. You ain't seen nothing yet!" It was boiling hot outside.

The bus driver welcomed us onboard with the words, "Welcome to our hot Washington DC!" I told him I had been caught quite unaware by the intensely humid air and everyone said the same thing. He laughed and said he heard that every day but that we would soon get used to it. His bus was, however, nicely air-conditioned and the ride to the hotel was smooth. I had picked up instructions for my direction from the airport and was able to find my way to the hotel with no difficulty.

The next morning, I took a cab to Georgetown University and was ushered into the office of the director of the School of Linguistics, who said I had just arrived on time as classes had just started a few days earlier. I met a Cameroonian student I knew who was already studying translation and interpretation for a year, and he was of great help to me. He took me to the students' residence to which I had been assigned, but warned me that it was quite expensive and that I may need to relocate, as he had done, to an apartment off campus, an advice I took to heart. At the end of the month, I moved to a much cheaper apartment in the neighbouring city of Arlington, in the State of Virginia, across the Potomac River, within walking distance of Georgetown. Arlington is famous for its military cemetery where President John F. Kennedy, the 35th President of the United States, and his other family members are buried. I became a regular visitor to that cemetery during the two years I spent in Washington, DC. I was particularly fascinated by the changing of the guards ceremony at the Tomb of the Unknown Soldier, especially the elaborate ceremony involved and the near robotic movements of the guards and the exact steps they took from one end to the other. It was a marvel to behold.

＊＊

One beautiful memory I have of my two-year stint in Washington DC is my immersion in the world of poetry reading. It happened quite unexpectedly. I was in my room playing with the dial of my transistor radio when I suddenly heard beautiful Congolese music from one of the stations. Then a voice came on shortly to announce that I was listening to "African Hour" on Pacifica Radio. It was a distinctly African voice which invited listeners to call in and talk. I did just that as soon as I had jotted down the phone number. I identified myself and said I was glad to listen to African music in Washington DC, of all places. When I heard I could also read my creative work on the air, I dropped the receiver and reached for a folder with some of my poems in it. I had been writing poems in Paris which I shared with Henry Bongasu Kishani and found his feedback very helpful. I called back Pacifica Radio and read some of them, which the host thought were beautiful. In fact, one listener, with a heavy Afro-American accent, called shortly thereafter to congratulate me on what I had just read. "That brother is so cool, man! That's awesome, man! I love it!" he said and I felt good. I then became a regular contributor to the weekly poetry reading. The "African Hour" host was a young man from Senegal, Cheikh Soumareh. He invited me to join him on the programme because he thought I could make a good addition to their team. Even though Pacifica was a mainly Jazz radio station, it also gave airtime to Africa and the Caribbean.

My love for the radio, which has lasted a lifetime, began on Pacifica Radio. My presence there enabled me to meet many Jazz musicians as well. When any of them was coming to the city, we would announce their arrival and open the lines for people to say what they knew about them. Whoever gave the correct answer to questions about a musician, received a free ticket to their show. The favourite jazz hub was the "Blues Alley" in the Georgetown neighbourhood. Those of us working at the radio station were given free tickets for the jazz shows.

I would often spend my afternoons after classes listening to the grand masters of Jazz. Pacifica Radio had them all lined up for your enjoyment: Charlie Parker; Dexter Gordon; Betty Carter; Miles Davis, yes, Miles, what an accomplished artist! Then the incomparable Louis Armstrong, "Satchmo," to the jazz connoisseur, with his deep, guttural voice screaming 'What a wonderful world!' Dizzy Gillespie, the trumpet wizard with inflated jaws, would chime in; so would Billy Holliday, that lady who sings the blues with such a haunting, tragedy-laden voice, and wails over strange fruits hanging from trees, a reference to blacks lynched in the southern part of America by the dreaded Ku Klux Klan. Then Nina Simone would make her dramatic appearance on the piano. Oh, what a lady! How tall and proud she stood as she violently castigated the society that could so cruelly eliminate such great souls as Malcolm X and Martin Luther King, Junior! "The King is dead!" she shouted before packing her bag and heading for France, which she made her home. From Canada, would come Oscar Peterson, that huge jazz musician, born in Montreal, a real monster on the piano, whom a critic once described as a man with a near flawless virtuosity. Wow!

I would listen as those musicians searched deep into the depths of their souls, marching across the Middle Passage, fondling the blood-stained walls of the infamous slave-forts studding the West African coastline, including Bimbia, in my homeland, all the way to the coast lands of Ghana and onto Gorée, off the coast of Senegal. With them, I would take the heart-rending voyage through 400 years of history, four long centuries of humiliation characterised by the whiplash and the searing cane lashes in the cotton, tobacco and sugarcane plantations of the Americas and the West Indies; yes, through four hundred long, tragic years of history, those jazz men and women would desperately search for their lost Africa.

The icing on the cake was when I was invited, among other poets, to read my poems to a public of poetry enthusiasts. Before long, I received an invitation from the publishers of a black magazine called "Nethula", which published two of my poems. Another black journal in New York also published a poem and a prose piece I wrote celebrating the return to one's country and to one's own roots. Those were the days when Alex Haley had just taken the literary and cinema world by storm with his saga of an American family which he wrote in 1976 entitled *Roots*. Many major television channels carried the captivating story of Kunta Kinte, an 18th century African, captured as an adolescent in the Gambia and transported to North America.

One good thing Alex Haley's family saga did for the African artistic scene was that it opened doors to many West African traditional poets, musicians and storytellers to come to the United States. There was renewed interest in the tradition of oral history as recounted by the 'griots', as the oral poets in many parts of West Africa are called. It was thanks to one such poet that Alex Haley was able to trace his roots to the Gambia. I had the singular delight of attending many of the performances of the visiting 'griots' in many packed halls in the Washington DC area.

I also remember meeting some African musicians of repute, notably two South Africans, Hugh Masekela and Dollar Brand, the latter having converted to Islam, taking the name Abdullah Ibrahim. He was huge on the piano. Hugh Masekela was already a name that floated liberally through the music scene in the United States. He was a trumpeter, a singer, and a composer, who quickly earned the name "the father of South African jazz."

I also met some African political leaders and personalities. Two of them come to mind: Jonas Savimbi of Angola and Ahmed Sekou Touré of Guinea Konakry. The American political establishment was hoisting Jonas Savimbi on the pedestal as a true African nationalist that was then blocking communism from consuming the entire continent of Africa. The reality in the black community in the Washington DC area told a totally different story. Placards appeared wherever Savimbi was rumoured to be, loudly denouncing him as a traitor, a war monger, among other unflattering titles. He was due to address the press one afternoon, but the hostility to his presence was so intense that he wisely opted not to attend. He instead sent one of his lieutenants who was so loudly booed by protestors banging on desks and shouting obscenities at him that security decided it was better to get him out alive, which they did by rushing him out of the hall through the back door.

Ahmed Sekou Touré, on the other hand, received a favourable welcome from the black community. I remember that he was given an enthusiastic hearing at Howard University. Amid sustained applause, he beamed a broad smile as he walked up to the podium. The presenter called him a hero and lauded his courage for being the only French-speaking African leader to have dared to challenge General De Gaulle and sent the French packing from his homeland. There was, however, a small group of noisy critics who held a brief protest at one corner of the campus, accusing Sekou Touré of gross human rights violations, but few paid any attention to their howls and drum-beatings. I stopped near them for a few minutes and heard them loudly denouncing Sekou Toure's iron-fisted rule in his country. They tried to make me sign a petition against his presence at Howard but I quickly fled from the scene, making my way to the hall to join his admirers.

CHAPTER 13

CANADA WELCOMES ME - 1980

After two years at Georgetown University, I wondered whether to go back to Cameroon or enrol in a doctoral programme at Howard University where I had been taking a few courses already. However, a phone call one afternoon led me to a destination I had not dreamt of - Canada. The phone call was from the Canadian city of Edmonton, in the province of Alberta. The caller identified himself as Steven Arnold, Professor of Comparative Literature at the University of Alberta. He said he knew I did not know him but that my brother, Kenjo Jumbam, had given him my phone number. Professor Arnold had just returned from Cameroon where he had met and interviewed my brother, among other writers. It was in the course of their discussion that my brother talked to him about me and that I, too, was dabbling in creative writing. He had promised to call me once back in Canada and had lived up to his promise.

We maintained a steady stream of correspondences over a period of several months. In one of them, he said he could get me a stipend that would enable me to undertake doctoral studies in Comparative Literature, if I so wished. That was a godsent opportunity I did not want to miss, especially as it would enable me to bring my fiancée, Maika, over to North America. We had been away from each other for some years and she was eagerly waiting for me to come back home so we could start a family. My study visa in the United States did not permit me to stay much longer after my studies. I discussed the matter with her and she agreed that it would be great for her too to pursue her studies for a higher degree in Canada. She had graduated from the University of Yaounde a year earlier and was teaching English to high school students at the Government Bilingual High School in Ngaoundere in the north of Cameroon. I called Professor Arnold, thanked him for his offer and said I was taking it. A week later, I received the necessary application forms for admission into the University of Alberta, Department of Comparative Literature. A favourable response came a week later.

With my admission letter warm in my pocket, I went to the Canadian embassy where I was issued a student visa. I bought an air ticket, packed my bag and flew out of Dulles International Airport for Edmonton via Chicago O'Hare. I remember spending a good number of hours at O'Hare waiting for a connecting flight by Air Canada. I arrived in Edmonton in late December in the thick of winter. Snow, several layers thick, covered the ground and coated the whole city in white. I had never seen so much concentration of snow in one place before. Professor Arnold and one of his daughters, Safi, were waiting for me. His family graciously hosted me for a few weeks, enough time for me to find a suitable place of my own.

The first year in Edmonton was a trying one for me. I had never felt as isolated and lonely as I felt then, mainly because of the weather. It was not too bad when it was snowing; the problem was when it stopped snowing and the freezing wind swept down on the city from the Rocky Mountains to the west. I was there for just a few months when we drove to Gainesville, Florida, for the yearly meeting of the African Literature Association (ALA) which, as the name suggests, is an association of scholars and students of African literature. Professor Steve Arnold was then the editor of that association's publication, "The African Literature Association Bulletin". Abioseh (Oseh) Porter, a fellow doctoral student from the West African country of Sierra Leone, was with us. I recall that he and his wife, Mulsie, had tied the knot just a few weeks before I arrived in Edmonton. Steve, in one of his letters, had expressed regret that I would not be in Edmonton early enough to attend their wedding. They have since remained life-long friends of our family.

We drove from Edmonton to Florida and back and it turned out to be the longest and most tiring journey I ever made. It took us over three days of sometimes driving day and night, only stopping in inns for a rub down and breakfast. We made a stopover in Kentucky for a day and took the occasion to visit one of the numerous caves for which that State is famous. The truly scary part was when we were inside the cave and our guide wanted us to feel what it would be like in the dark. He turned off the lights and we all gasped in terror for the darkness was truly deep and frightening. He then asked us to imagine how the native Americans, the original inhabitants of that region, had been able to explore that cave sometimes with just torches made from wood. When he turned back the lights on, the group expressed an audible gasp of relief. We then went on the exploration of the cave and must have travelled over a mile inside, sometimes literally crawling on all fours through the narrow paths that led to the exit at the other end. When we finally emerged in the open, everyone heaved a sigh of relief. A good thing we did not have to go back the reverse way as a bus was waiting to take us back to our car. It was an experience that has lived with me all my life.

In Gainesville, I met many literary critics of African literature whose works I had read. It was a delight to meet them in flesh and blood. I also met and talked with some African writers, who had been invited to the conference, among whom was Francis Bebey from my country, Cameroon, who also doubled as a musician. He was given space to showcase his musical talents and he also actively participated in the discussion on Cameroon literature since he was directly mentioned in many of the presentations.

I also met Dennis Brutus, South African poet and anti-Apartheid activist who had spent jail time in his country for his opposition to his country's politics of Apartheid. Like many of his country men and women, who opposed the government, he was living in exile in the United States.

The icing on the cake came from the presence of Chinua Achebe of Nigeria. His name had been on everyone's lips when word had gone round that he was around and would be present during the closing ceremony. He appeared on the stage with the Afro-American writer James Baldwin. I recall that as Baldwin was greeting what he called 'my brother whom I haven't met in 400 years', a hate-filled voice suddenly broke through the intercom system, asking James Baldwin to take his 'niggers' out of town; and that if he did not, those making the threats would run them out themselves. That was scary! The atmosphere, that had been quite convivial and cheerful, suddenly dampened as an eerie feeling gripped the hall. James Baldwin skipped to his feet and loudly challenged those white supremacists to come and get him. When Chinua Achebe took the floor, he pleaded for tolerance among all races, referring to our common humanity as reason not to spread racism and hatred. For that, he received a standing ovation.

It was a week of intense activity as I moved from one panel to another, listening to high quality presentations from renowned critics of African literature, some of them having travelled all the way from Africa, although the majority of them were teaching in many North American and Canadian universities. There were also writers and literary critics from the Caribbean who gave another spice to the discussions. Through them, I discovered another dimension of the African literary reality, that of Africa in the dispersion.

After the conference, we again set out on the road, driving up the east coast of the United States, stopping for a night in Washington, DC, to visit Steve Arnold's brother. I was able to re-connect with some folks I had left there barely six months earlier.

A year after my arrival in Edmonton, Maika, my fiancée joined me. Her presence changed my life completely. It brought much stability which I was not even aware my life needed. Where at first I would leave my room without knowing when I would be coming back, I now knew when I happened to be out by myself that there was someone waiting for me at home and I would hurry back to be with her. No more late-night parties; no more knocking on others' doors at night just for a drink. It was strange at first but with time, it all became routine and natural.

Prior to Maika's arrival in Edmonton, I never went to church. I had for years considered myself an irremediably fallen Catholic Christian. I did not even pretend that salvation was anything I could strive for anymore. Whenever religious memories popped to mind, I would quickly dismiss them as sheer relics of my boyhood years. But, no sooner had she arrived than she asked me where the nearest Catholic church was and was visibly stunned when I told her I had no idea and that, in fact, I had never even thought of it.

Our first quarrel as a couple began over my rather lukewarm attitude towards my faith, a sharp contrast to hers, which was still warm and alive. At first, I thought it was because she had just arrived from home and that the freezing cold of the Canadian winter would dampen it sooner rather than later; but I was wrong. She found out where the nearest Catholic church was and made it a duty not to miss the Sunday mass, the freezing weather being no obstacle.

I remember a phone call we received one winter night announcing the death of my sister-in-law, Gertrude, my brother Kenjo's wife. Kenjo had just gone back home from the University of Laval in Quebec, where he had just completed his studies, when the shocking news of Gertrude's death hit us. I could not sleep all that night. Early the next morning, which was a Sunday, Maika announced that I was going to follow her to church. "Even if the devil has truly made his home in your soul," she said, "on a day like this, you should go to church and pray for the eternal repose of your sister-in-law's soul. It is either that, or there will be no food for you in this house today!"

The fear of starvation had an immediate effect. I stood up reluctantly, dressed and trudged behind her to church, where I grudgingly sat wondering when the priest was going to shut up so I would go back home to a good afternoon lunch and rest. When the Mass was finally over, I heaved a sigh of relief and headed for the door, barely stopping to greet some friends Maika had made in church, and who were eager to meet her husband. As they pressed around me wondering why I was not coming to church with my wife, I promised I would make it a point to accompany her, but that was just to get them off my back. I had no intention of ever going back there again, threats of food starvation notwithstanding.

Before long, however, letters started coming from home with practically the same message: "When are you two going to get married in church?" I had been expecting such letters but it was the sheer volume coming from both families that stunned me. Maika's father reminded me that he had not sent his daughter to me as my concubine. We needed to bless our union in the presence of a church minister and that they were waiting to see the wedding pictures. Similar messages poured in from my own family. I started feeling that a family conspiracy was being hatched against me, and Maika watched the drama with a satisfied smile on her lips.

I finally yielded to family pressure and, for the first time in decades, I found myself standing before a priest listening to him talk about the sacrament of holy matrimony. As he spoke, I stood there wondering if I really needed to hear advice of how to live my marriage life from someone who was not even married! In silence, I meekly submitted myself to the torture. For over a week, we had been attending doctrine classes that were crowned by confession. I recall going down on my knees in a confessional, trying to figure out what to tell the priest concerning my life as a fallen Christian. Where could I start, given that there were layers and layers of sins that had accumulated and hardened in every corner of my soul. As I knelt there, the scare I had felt as a kid kneeling before our parish priest, Fara Nji, over three decades earlier, resurfaced. I saw myself again an eight-year-old boy fumbling before a priest and imagining what I thought were sins. The story was not much different from my childhood days and I was only too happy to flee as soon as it was over.

Maika and I agreed on the wedding day, and she made all the arrangements with the parish priest, who was to officiate at the ceremony. Our Cameroonian friends, Linus and Therese Asong, served as our witnesses. A few days before the wedding, Linus and I went hunting for our wedding rings. Those things cost a fortune but we were lucky to find a jewellery store run by an Ethiopian who sold them to us at a reasonable price. The wedding proper was a simple one. We were less than ten of us in a small chapel and I was surprised at how fast it all went. I had not thought I would feel so good afterwards, but I did. I began to feel that we were now truly a married couple.

The feeling of responsibility intensified when Simolen, our daughter, was born. When Maika was pregnant, I accompanied her on all medical check-ups with the obstetrician. We also attended pre-natal classes together. I was glad I took those lessons to heart because I learnt a great deal about women and pregnancy and the physical and especially the mood swings that had baffled me so much. It was amazing watching the videos of women giving birth and learning how important it truly was for the man to be present at that critical moment in his wife's life when she was bringing a new life to the world.

When the delivery day came, we left the house as soon as the contractions were already becoming frequent. We followed all the instructions given during the sessions with the midwives. I was a nervous wreck as I saw the contractions becoming more and more frequent and I knew it would not be long before Maika was delivered of our first child, boy or girl. We had been told that we could always ask and know our baby's sex before delivery, but we disagreed. We wanted a healthy child, whether boy or girl.

As Maika was being whisked into the labour room, I was glad I could stand by her and hold her hand and clean sweat off her forehead as she lay on the delivery table. The obstetrician lifted our baby up and said aloud, "It's a girl," and then placed her on a small table nearby where one of the attending nurses started the cleaning process. Simolen did not make any noise and I remember Maika, who could not see what was going on, becoming alarmed. She asked why she was not making any noise and I assured her that she was well. One of the nurses laughed and said anyone who had made such a long journey could be excused for not having the strength to cry. I watched in amazement as the nurse dangled some keys back and forth over my daughter's eyes and I could see those bright eyes following the movements of the keys back and forth. The tears I had been holding back popped out of my eyes for that was truly a moment of intense emotions for me. I watched as the nurse wrapped my daughter in clean clothes and put a tag number on her tiny wrist with Maika's name on it. What a treasure she was!

* * *

One of the first things I did when I arrived in Edmonton was to go to the university students' radio station CJSR where the station manager and his team received me. They were pleasantly surprised by my offer, which was to kickstart a radio programme entirely dedicated to Africa. No one before me had thought of involving the African community in the activities of the radio. That was understandable given that the African community on campus constituted a minor presence as compared to students from other parts of the world – China, Korea and Japan, for example. Diversity, or what was known in city hall as "multi-culturalism," was not a word one heard often in the university environment, and so when I offered to put some African sound and voice in the airwaves of the city of Edmonton through the campus radio, my offer was warmly received. As a precaution, however, I was asked to record at least three programmes of one hour each to prove that "African Hour," which was the name I gave to it, would last. I did not only produce the three programmes they initially asked for, I did five and they all received rave reviews from the team. It was something new and listeners seemed to like it, at least from the numerous phone calls the programme began to receive shortly after it hit the airwaves of the city.

Before long, many African students were coming forward to talk to me on the air about their studies, their family lives in Edmonton, and what they were missing about their home countries. Canadians too, especially the few who had travelled to, or lived in Africa, accepted my invitation to share their African experiences on the air. My programme soon caught the attention of the folks of City Hall and I was invited to some meetings where multi-culturalism, that was then beginning to make inroads into the vocabulary of many politicians in the city, was the main subject of discussion. I was given access to information that could be of benefit to the African community. One day, I was scared when I arrived at the studio and was told the police had come looking for me. I just could not figure out what it was I might have done wrong. That was a few months before Maika joined me and I felt terribly lonely and frightened.

Some friends, to whom I discussed my fear of the police, gave me all kinds of advice that made me even more scared. Some thought I should not talk to the cops in the absence of a lawyer. But then the services of a lawyer, as I found out, were not cheap. A few days later, the cops were back when I was on the air. As I stepped out of the studio, I saw two of them waiting for me. They must have seen the look of fright in my face for they smiled, shook my trembling hand, and said they had been sitting at the lobby listening to my programme, which they said was quite 'exotic'. They then congratulated me on what they said was a wonderful tool of communication that was giving a very positive side to the African presence, not only on campus, but in the entire city of Edmonton. The sigh of relief I heaved must have been heard miles away. They asked to know if I had any objection to receiving and interviewing some members of the police force who could use my programme to reach out to the African community, not only on campus but throughout the city of Edmonton. They just wanted an interview to let the African community know that the police were there to protect, not brutalise them. Was I open to their proposal? I said that was perfectly good by me and we agreed when the first interview would be. I called one of our technicians and we agreed when to do the recording and so began a series of talks with the Edmonton police in which they basically urged Africans to feel free in the city, to consider the police as their friends, not their adversary, and to abide by the laws of the country that was hosting them.

My collaboration with the police was not without its detractors, especially in the African student community. Some thought I was a mere collaborator with the police with the purpose of spying on Africans. One such detractor, who happened to be from my home country, Cameroon, insisted that I prove to him that I was not working for the Canadian secret service, or for the American CIA, since I had lived in Washington DC. He claimed he knew my type and that I had better keep my distance from him because I was not someone to trust. I decided he was not worth the trouble and ignored him although that did not stop him from his campaign of denigration that found echo among Africans of like minds. One day, I even invited him and a few of his friends to come on the air and tell listeners why it was such a bad idea for the African community to listen to the police. His reaction was immediate, "You see, now he wants me to implicate myself by criticising the cops so I can be thrown out of the country! Look for your victim somewhere else!" he spat out and walked away. His mind was already made up and nothing I could say or do could make him think otherwise, so I decided to ignore him altogether.

* * *

One of the memories I latch onto and cherish so much was an invitation I received to attend a workshop on creative teaching at the University of Toronto in Ontario. One day, to my utter surprise, I received a phone call from a woman, named Liz Cockburn. I had never heard of her before. She said Kenjo, my brother, who was then studying at Laval University in Quebec, had given her my phone number. She lightened the discussion by telling me about the many years she and her husband had spent teaching in a college in Cameroon, precisely in Bambui, Bamenda. During her stay in Cameroon, she had worked with many women's groups, encouraging adult literacy and other developmental projects that could help the women improve their status. She was also keen on helping teachers in primary school improve their teaching methods so they could become better teachers for their pupils.

When her family returned to Canada, she had enrolled in the department of English at Guelph where the Chair, Professor Dough Killam, was her teacher. By chance, she met Professor Bernard Nsokika Fonlon, Chair of the Department of African and Afro-American Studies at the University of Yaounde, whom she had heard so much about during her stay in Cameroon, but had never met in person. He had come to Guelph at Professor Killam's invitation as part of his department's strategy to foster relations with the Department of African and Afro-American Studies of the University of Yaounde under Professor Fonlon. The two men were already long-standing friends. From their discussions, in which Liz was allowed to sit in, a project called "The Guelph-Yaoundé Project" was born.

The new project also gave birth to what came to be known as the "Association for Creative Teaching (ACT)," which involved encouraging school children and their teachers at the primary school level to engage in creating their own works. The teachers were coached on ways of leading their pupils to write their own stories that would then be edited and published in booklet forms for use as teaching material throughout the schools.

She was inviting me to join my brother and some English-speaking Cameroonians for a week of brainstorming on ways and means of improving the teaching of creative writing at the primary school level in northwest and southwest regions of Cameroon. I gladly accepted her invitation and we spent a week at the University of Toronto discussing writing by children and for children at the primary school level. That was a totally new area for me and it made me appreciate just how challenging it was assessing stories written by and for children.

One year later, I was again invited to attend another workshop still on the Association for Creative Teaching project. Whereas a year earlier only one person had come from Cameroon, Mr. Patrick Mbunwe, this time around, Professor Bernard Fonlon would be coming at the head of a delegation from Yaounde. A number of other Cameroonian students studying in Canada and the United States would also be present. I informed Liz that my participation was contingent upon Maika and our seven-month-old daughter, Simolen, accompanying me. A day later, she called to say that she had discussed my proposal with the other organisers and that my family was welcome. She asked me for details of our identification as they featured on our travel documents and then said I should go to the Air Canada office in downtown Edmonton the next day where our tickets would be waiting for us.

For a week, we attended the workshop with about ten other participants under the guidance of Professors Fonlon and Killam and Liz Cockburn. Maika too took an active part in the workshop and arrangements were made for someone to baby-sit our daughter. It was a great learning experience for us all and I came to see just how difficult it is to write for children. Their books may look simply written but the author needs to come down to their level and see the world through their own eyes to be able to write for them or appreciate how they see the world around them. It was, however, an experience I greatly appreciated.

**

One of the highlights of the week was the surprise appearance of the incomparable Nigerian writer Chinua Achebe. He and Professor Fonlon had been friends for long and were on first-name basis. Professor Doug Killam had invited Chinua to spend some time with him in Guelph, which coincided with our workshop.

I felt particularly privileged that our paths were crossing for the second time in three years. I had seen him from a distance at the African Literature Association conference in Gainesville, Florida, in 1980. This time I was meeting him face-to-face. He would occasionally drop in to wish us well and share a thought or two before gently withdrawing to his room. The last day, we all came together in one room and Professors Killam and Fonlon took their seats at a table in front of us. They then asked Chinua, who had been sitting among us, to take the empty seat between them. He reluctantly left his seat and walked up to the front, slightly protesting that he was more a 'gate-crasher' among us than a real participant. We all laughed and clapped as he took the seat reserved for him.

Professor Killam then placed a tape-recorder before him but he immediately recoiled from it, telling us that each time this thing, he pointed to the tape-recorder, came out, he always went blank and never knew what to say. We all laughed and clapped again as he relaxed into his seat. He then lauded the collaborative efforts of the Universities of Yaounde and Guelph to promote creative teaching in English-speaking Cameroonian schools, beginning at the primary school level. He fielded questions from the audience, which mainly centred around his writing career. There was much empathy in the room as he answered each question clearly, occasionally spicing it with humour that sent the audience laughing and clapping. He was a man of palpable humility, gentle in speech and even in the way he moved about.

I still value the copy of his book, *A Man of the People*, which he autographed for me. We were not able to find a copy of his books anywhere in Guelph and Liz Cockburn graciously gave me her copy in which Chinua Achebe wrote some kind words before appending his signature and the date below. You could not come face-to-face with him and ever forget his easy smile, as well as his gentle and unassuming ways. Such meetings hardly leave any student of literature unmoved. It left a lasting impression on me.

One week later, we were back in Edmonton just on time to receive a call from an official of the Cameroon High Commission in Ottawa, announcing the arrival in the city of Edmonton of our country's High Commissioner. Could I do everything possible to assemble the Cameroonian community to meet him? The call came from a young diplomat who had spent a week in the city of Edmonton some months earlier and a few of us had met him for informal discussions. The Cameroonian community then was made up of less than ten persons consisting of a few families and some single students. Unlike the Cameroonian diplomats I had had the misfortune to meet elsewhere, especially in Madrid, the young man had been very cordial in his ways. He said the High Commissioner had sent him on a mission to the different provinces of Canada to find out how Cameroonians were faring and how we thought the High Commission could better serve us. That was new language to my ears. I had never thought someone from our diplomatic representation could be so open in his dealings with us. He left a good impression on all who listened to him.

When he called, he informed me that the High Commissioner had been happy with the openness with which we had received him and was planning to come for a visit himself. He gave me the name of the hotel where the High Commissioner, His Excellency Lucas Aza Kemta and his wife, would be in and when they would be arriving. I immediately contacted the few Cameroonians around and we all agreed to meet him. My friend, Linus Asong, a writer in his own right and a fellow doctoral student in my department, helped review the short welcome speech I had written for the occasion. I was selected to read it on behalf of the group.

The High Commissioner turned out to be a pleasant gentleman to talk with. He was already a man of a certain age and spoke to us in a very fatherly tone of voice, cracking jokes and switching from English to Pidgin at will, which further spiced our discussions and brought them down to earth. We had been expecting to meet an arrogant, high-sounding diplomat ready to lord it over us. We were all on our guard but the fatherly man we met disarmed us by his gentle ways. His wife immediately invited the women to join her in the kitchen to bring out food for the tables. She then literally ordered Linus and me to uncork the wine bottles and bring the wine glasses from a table at the corner. "Don't expect the women to do all the work for you while you sit and only wait to eat, you fellows!" she said as she dashed in and out of the kitchen. Her husband laughed and said, "You people haven't seen anything yet. If you were not here, I would be the one running around at her command." We all burst out laughing, which further eased communication in the room. The hotel had prepared what turned out to be quite a sumptuous lunch for us and we spent a good afternoon with the diplomat and his wife.

CHAPTER 14

HOME, SWEET HOME! - 1984

One of the things the High Commissioner reiterated, which his assistant had raised during his visit, was the High Commission's openness to assist Cameroonians willing to return to Cameroon by paying their flight home. About a year later, when Maika and I decided it was time to go back home, I contacted the High Commission in Ottawa to let them know we were ready to take their repatriation offer. Would they pay our way back home? I was asked to speak to the young diplomat, who had visited us earlier in the year, and he was glad to know that we had decided to go back home. He said all arrangements would be made for my family to travel back home safely. A week after my phone call, he called and said our air tickets were waiting for us at the Air Canada office. What a pleasant surprise!

A few months before we left Canada, Professor Steve Arnold and Abioseh (Oseh) Porter and I attended the African Studies Association (ASA) conference in the city of Calgary. There we met Professor Bernard Fonlon, who had been invited as a special guest from the University of Yaounde. He took time in between sessions to receive me and I remember informing him that I was already preparing to go back home. Even though I had completed my residency requirements for a doctorate degree, and all that was left was the thesis, I did not want to spend at least two more years on it. I was already exhausted and home sick. I had been out of Cameroon for ten years already and I needed to go back home, get a job and raise a family. He said he understood me and that he was open to enrolling me in his department where I could continue my research work that would enable me to complete my thesis; after which I could then return for the defence in Edmonton. It all sounded good to my ears and Steve Arnold was also pleased with that option. Steve wrote a beautifully worded letter of recommendation for me, which he titled "All But Dissertation (ABD)," telling whoever it may concern that I was a hard-working student, who had completed all the requirements for the award of a Ph.D. in Comparative Literature from the University of Alberta, and all that remained was to complete my thesis, hence the title, "All But Dissertation (ABD)."

We flew out of Edmonton one bright sunny morning in the month of July 1984. We had a stopover of a few hours in Montreal, Quebec, before the long haul to Paris. We arrived just on time for our connecting flight by Cameroon Airlines to Douala. As soon as we took our seats, I knew we were back home. The volume of laughter and animated discussions prior to departure, and throughout the flight, showed me we were back home. Then the rudeness of the air hostesses was such a sharp contrast to the air hostesses aboard Air Canada, and that too was a clear indication – hard to accept -- that we were surely back home. On Air Canada, the hostesses wore smiles on their faces and always had a sweet word for our daughter each time they came around. They had no problem letting me eat first while Maika took care of Simolen; then I would in turn take care of her while Maika's food was served. Aboard Cameroon Airlines, however, hardly any hostess smiled and one of them was particularly disagreeable. When she came to serve us, I asked if she could serve me first and Maika later. She did not only refuse but was quite vocal about it, speaking out loud, for everyone around to hear, about how unreasonable some people could be. Did I not know that there was a time to eat and a time for them to collect the dishes? At one moment, she even shouted at Maika when Simolen was restlessly pushing things around: "*Vous ne pouvez pas bien tenir votre enfant là, Madame.*" [Can't you take care of your baby, Madam?] Before walking away, a frown on her face, she muttered something about women who gave birth to babies and could not take care of them, and I even heard people who thought what she said was funny. It was a patience-taxing experience, which showed us that we were truly back home.

A year after our return home, our first son, Loayeh, was born. I was still in the job market, wearing out the bottom of my shoes as I trudged from one office to another in desperate search of a job to feed my growing family. Money was tight and we felt relieved when my brother, Lawrence, asked that I bring Maika and Simolen to his home in Bambili so she could be delivered of our second child in Bamenda; and that is what we did. Communication being as poor as it then was between Yaounde and Bamenda, with no easy access to the phone, it was only two days after my son's birth that I received a hand-delivered message from my brother informing me of the good news. I arrived to find Loayeh and his mother already resting at home and together we gave thanks to God for another precious gift to our family. My regret, however, was that I had not been present to accompany Maika to the delivery room as I had done when Simolen came into the world.

Some years later, when Maika was again expecting, we were all in Douala with stable jobs and I was determined not to be deprived of the joy of assisting at the birth of our last child. The delivery day came and I drove Maika to the hospital. We did not have long to wait before she was taken to the delivery room. As I followed her into the delivery room, one of the midwives stopped me at the door, telling me I could not go in with her. I said I wanted to be present as my child was being delivered. I thought she was going to congratulate me on my move but she instead sent out a shrieking cry: "You say weti, papa? You wan go see how your woman di born. My mamie-eeh! Make wuna come hear me badlok! Man pickin say i wan go see how i woman di born-eeeh!! Na badlok dis?"

Before long, I was surrounded by other midwives and nurses and I could hear doors to wards on that floor flinging open and heads popping out to better see the man who wanted to go into the delivery room with his wife. I was truly stunned and I did not know what to say or do. One of the nurses asked me what my true intentions were since I was insisting to be allowed in the delivery room where my wife was in labour. I told her I thought it was my right to be present at the birth of my child. What was so criminal about that? I asked. For an answer, she let out another shriek, asking out loud why a man who never let his wife sleep at night should now come to disturb midwives, who were trying to relieve the poor woman of the load he had burdened her with? "Some man pikin no get shame at-all, at-all!" she said, to much laughter from the others. You could have thought I was just a sex pervert who had been caught pants down committing a lewd act. "Na my woman, no?" I asked. "Yes, na ya woman. You don givam belle and you wan come see how ih di born? Na which kind badlok dat?" she asked, and the growing crowd of nurses and patients, who had come out to see and hear what was going on, burst out in laughter.

I wondered since when impregnating one's lawfully married wife had become an offence in this country. With mockery and laughter and unprintable remarks making the rounds of that floor, I had no choice but to take a seat at a corner, waiting for my son's delivery. And that was how I was deprived of the joy of assisting at the delivery of my second boy, Kiwo. I was truly back in Cameroon.

ACKNOWLEDGMENTS

I am grateful to my wife, Maika, and my children, Simolen, Loayeh and Kiwo, for making our home a happy place to come back to after a whole day at work. They have always endured my long hours when I hermetically lock myself away in a separate room, especially in the early morning hours, without which much of the writing I have done over the years would not have been possible. I thank them for their understanding and support.

I also express my gratitude to a number of friends, who insisted that I write this memoir:

A family friend, Professor Michael Abioseh Porter, a Sierra Leonean colleague from our University of Alberta days in the 1980s. Our families have since remained friends and he continually reminded me of what he calls "my rich background of travels throughout the world" that merited to be documented in a memoir.

My friend, Dibussi Tande, a Cameroonian blogger, and a renowned poet and political commentator, did not only insist on my writing this memoir but took the pain and the time to revise the final product.

Professor Jude Fokwang of Spears Media Press had an irresistible way of gently prodding me on to write my memoir and this product is, to a large extent, the result of his encouraging reminders.

ABOUT THE AUTHOR

Martin Jumbam holds a bilingual (English/French) degree from the University of Yaounde, Cameroon, a diploma in Spanish studies from La Universidad Complùtense in Madrid, Spain, a Maîtrise en littérature comparée from La Sorbonne Nouvelle, Paris 3; a diploma in translation/interpretation from Georgetown University in Washington DC, and a Master's Degree in Comparative Literature from the University of Alberta in Edmonton, Canada. He worked for over 20 years for an American oil company, Pecten Cameroon, in the port city of Douala, Cameroon, before serving for four years as the general manager of *La Maison Catholique de la Communication Sociale* (MACACOS), the Catholic Media House of the Archdiocese of Douala. He is the author of *My Conversion Journey with Christian Cardinal Tumi* (Langaa Publishing, 2014), *Beads of Memory* (Spears Books, 2020), and co-author of *My Night in Captivity* (Spears Books 2021), a memoir by the late Emeritus Archbishop of the Catholic

Archdiocese of Douala in Cameroon, Christian Cardinal Wiyghan Tumi that details his one-night ordeal in the hands of separatist forces in Ndop in the restive North West region of Cameroon in 2019. He lives in Douala and works as a freelance translator, conference interpreter, journalist and motivational speaker.

ABOUT THE PUBLISHER

Spears Books is an independent publisher dedicated to providing innovative publication strategies with emphasis on African/Africana stories and perspectives. As a platform for alternative voices, we prioritize the accessibility and affordability of our titles in order to ensure that relevant and often marginal voices are represented at the global marketplace of ideas. Our titles – poetry, fiction, narrative nonfiction, memoirs, reference, travel writing, African languages, and young people's literature – aim to bring African worldviews closer to diverse readers. Our titles are distributed in paperback and electronic formats globally by African Books Collective.

Connect with Us: Go to www.spearsmedia.com to learn about exclusive previews and read excerpts of new books, find detailed information on our titles, authors, subject area books, and special discounts.

Subscribe to our Free Newsletter: Be amongst the first to hear about our newest publications, special discount offers, news about bestsellers, author interviews, coupons and more! Subscribe to our newsletter by visiting www.spearsmedia.com

Quantity Discounts: Spears Books are available at quantity discounts for orders of ten or more copies. Contact Spears Books at orders@spearsmedia.com.

Host a Reading Group: Learn more about how to host a reading group on our website at www.spearsmedia.com

www.ingramcontent.com/pod-product-compliance
Lightning Source LLC
Chambersburg PA
CBHW031223230426
43667CB00029BA/1390